COUNTRY LIVING BY
SEA AND ESTUARY

COUNTRY LIVING
BY SEA AND ESTUARY

SUZANNE BEEDELL

David & Charles
Newton Abbot London North Pomfret (Vt)

By the same author
Windmills
The Complete Guide to Country Living

British Library Cataloguing in Publication Data

Beedell, Suzanne
    Country living by sea and estuary.
    1. Country life – Great Britain – Dictionaries
    2. Coasts – Great Britain – Dictionaries
    3. Estuaries – Great Britain – Dictionaries
    941'.0094'6   S522.G7

ISBN 0–7153–7796–5

Typeset by Northampton Phototypesetters Ltd
and printed in Great Britain by Biddles Ltd Guildford
for David & Charles (Publishers) Limited
Brunel House   Newton Abbot   Devon

Published in the United States of America
by David & Charles Inc
North Pomfret   Vermont 05053   USA

Contents

1

The Sea and the Coastline

All life on earth is governed by the sun and the moon. As the earth moves spinning round the sun, life waxes and wanes with days and seasons, and as our own satellite the moon moves round earth, her gravitational pull controls the tides, and her waxing and waning seems to affect our physical lives and behaviour. For people living in towns and cities, these effects are smothered or diverted by all the other enormous pressures of modern life. Return to the country where the full moon is the brightest thing in the night sky, and not just a wishy-washy disc behind the metallic purple glow of the city lights, and she again becomes dominant. Walked upon, driven upon and orbited, photographed and carried away piecemeal in plastic bags, in fact generally scratched and tickled by inquisitive mankind, the moon remains aloof, beautiful and powerful.

To live by tidal water is to be aware of the power of the moon because the rhythms of the tides directly affect coastal life in all its forms. The movements of seabirds and waders as they flight in to feed on mudflat and saltmarsh; the passage of fish within the water, the passage of boats upon it; the onset of sea mist or of sea breezes; the actions of fisherman or wildfowler, of bait digger or cockleman; the sound of water when the tide is in, and the moving of sunlight or moonlight upon it; the stillness of mudflats, and the gleam of them full of reflections bright and dark by day and night.

As the tide falls, on steep beaches sucking and dragging everything back with it, each succeeding wave seeming more reluctant to rush up the beach, or on sand flats running back fast as if there was an open plug hole out there, and in saltmarshes slipping quietly away till water becomes mud, and wide rivers become creeks not deep or wide enough to float a pudding basin, there is a sense of respite and relief. Time to do the things that must be done before the sea returns, to dig

Moonlit water

bait or cockles, to repair and paint boats, to sort and mend nets and pots, to walk, to watch the birds, to paint pictures, to take photographs. And in settled weather, even the wind drops away with the tide.

As the tide rises, if you are on mud or sand flat, first there is a change in the look of the sea's edge. The small waves begin their relentless forward movement and throw little hard shadows so that the practised eye can tell the moment the tide is on the make. As the sea floods back, the creeks fill, and the water runs with little sucking noises across the mudflats, or clicks in sandy shingle. On steep shingle banks the note changes to an increasing crash and roar if the sea is rough, and if it is calm, to a persistent rough breathing as the sea advances. And the whole feeling changes to one of urgency. Time to put to sea, time to work or play upon the water. Time to worry about high tides and the damage they do. Time for the waders to move away from the waterline or the flats where they can no longer feed, and to flight inland or out to sea. The seagulls after whatever they can scavenge from boats and fishermen, and from drains and sewers, and terns hunting fish fry driven into shallow waters by marauding mackerel are noisy and urgent, and yachtsmen are happy now because they have water to sail on and a breeze has come up with the tide to go with it.

Tides

In Czechoslovakia someone asked me to explain to him how the tides and waves worked, and what they really looked like. He had never seen the sea, and films and photographs show nothing of the actual movement of the tides. Stand on a bank of the sea at dead low water, and the visible horizon is much further away from you than it is from the same viewpoint at high water. Eyes 8ft above sea level see the horizon at about $3\frac{1}{4}$ miles. Ships are clearly visible which would be hull down from the same viewpoint, or below the horizon, at high water. The actual range of tidal rise and fall varies throughout the world and even round the coasts of Britain varies from about 40ft in the Bristol Channel through about 15ft at Dover, to as little as 1ft at Southampton. Nevertheless all that enormous mass of water that you see out there at high tide flows off somewhere else for more than six hours, and then comes back again. To understand why this happens is not difficult, but to comprehend how is another matter.

Tides are caused by the gravitational pull of the moon. This makes two enormous bulges in the earth's water, one on the side directly facing the moon, and the other on the opposite side, caused it is believed by the earth itself being pulled away from the water. Between the two bulges the water level is lowered. The friction of the water against the earth beneath causes a time lag or drag so that high tide is not exactly beneath the moon, but lags behind a little. Were the whole surface of the earth nothing but water, these two enormous waves would travel round and round it making continuous tides, but this does not happen because of the land masses and the depressions in the

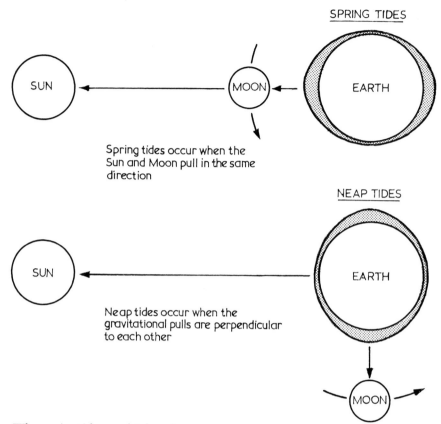

SPRING TIDES

SUN ← MOON ← EARTH

Spring tides occur when the
Sun and Moon pull in the same
direction

NEAP TIDES

SUN ← EARTH

Neap tides occur when the
gravitational pulls are perpendicular
to each other

MOON

Why springtides are higher than neaps

ocean floors and other factors which all affect the tides. Instead of one tide, there are many local tides, which, because the earth rotates, circle round centres or 'amphidromic points'. In the centre of each, there is almost no tide at all. An immense wave forms which circles round and round the points, anti-clockwise in the northern hemisphere. Such a circular movement includes the whole North Atlantic, giving us our west coast tides opposite to those of the Canadian seaboard. Our north-west coasts are affected by circular systems between the Mull of Kintyre and the coast of northern Ireland and between northern Scotland and Ireland. The east coast tides are formed by smaller circular movements in the North Sea, and off Denmark and southern Norway.

All this means that the tides round our coasts seem at first sight to obey no regular pattern and are extremely confusing for amateur navigators and others. High tide at Dover is taken as the norm or starting point and tide tables for our coasts are all worked out in terms of hours plus or minus high tide at Dover. The tides differ so much that, for instance, low tide in Cornwall is high tide time in Kent. If it is necessary for you to know the local tide times, tables can always be bought in fishing gear shops, sailing gear shops and many local newspapers give high tide times each week, and if you know the constant differential between your local high tide and Dover high tide time then it is easy to work out tides from a Dover tide table.

Of course, all that water rushing about creates tidal streams, and these are clearly marked on Admiralty charts and books of maps showing them at different states of the tide. This is very important for fishermen and sailors as tides can run so fast locally (normally between 1 and 3 knots, but occasionally up to 10 knots) that little headway may be made against them either by sail or power and it is far better to wait till the tide changes in your favour than to waste petrol or energy trying to beat it. Tidal streams may carry you towards danger and therefore should be carefully noted and avoided. The configuration of the bottom where there are sandbanks, overfalls and depressions, can create tidal streams which are only a few yards wide in places and which run much faster than surrounding water. Those who know a particular estuary or coast well can tell just by looking at the surface of the water and the way it is moving whereabouts they are. Over a shallow bank the surface may take on the look of runny boiling porridge as the tidal stream is interrupted by it, or where the bottom is suddenly a deep channel, the choppy surface runs like a river within the sea itself. Nowhere is the tidal stream more evident than where it passes a channel buoy or a pier. As unpredictable by rule of thumb as the tides themselves, tidal streams change direction as the tides change, lagging behind because it takes some time for the movements of enormous bodies of water to slow down, stop (slack water) and reverse direction.

The speed at which the tide ebbs or flows up or down the beach or in an estuary is affected by another factor, which is the gradient of the ground it covers. The shallower the beach, the faster the tide appears to cross it. There are places, such as Burnham on Sea and Weston-Super-Mare on the Bristol Channel, and the Solway Firth, where the sea disappears almost out of sight at low tide, and then, as it comes in, races up the beach. At half tide on such beaches you can wade out for hundreds of yards before the water comes above your waist. Usually the last few feet rise up much more steeply to deepen the whole sea area. Holkham in Norfolk is such a beach. Yet on a steep shingle bank,

Deal: half-tide

such as Deal in Kent, the width of the bank from high tide mark to low
is only 30 or 40 yards. In both places the actual rise of the water is about
15ft.

In estuaries, apart from the river channels, the water covers the
shallow mudflats very quickly once it has come into the mouth of the
estuary, and here other very important factors come into play. The
configuration of the bottom may at first be steep, and then suddenly,
inside the estuary, become shallower. This will cause the tide to build
up till it reaches the point where the bottom changes, and then sweep
forward very fast indeed, even creating a wave or bore, over the
shallower ground. Long narrow inlets where the water cannot escape
sideways exaggerate this phenomenon. Many harbours and estuaries
have bars; ridges of sand or mud are deposited where the outgoing
river meets the sea and its tides, and are worked by wind and water to
form a bank. This creates a barrier or series of barriers, which is always
overcome by a fierce rush of water as the tide comes in, and where
there will always be broken water in windy weather or when there is
any sea running, and dangerous swells for the boatman.

This formation of bars can completely close a harbour, as happened in the past at Blakeney in Norfolk – sandspits forming on the seaward side of the harbour eventually came right out of the water and formed ridges of dunes. These bars are still forming at Blakeney, out under the water off the point, as overfalls which create dangerous and turbulent tide races and rips, while the inside of the harbour is extremely shallow and only navigable by small yachts where only a few centuries ago was a thriving commercial port.

The wide estuary of the river Dee between Cheshire and Wales, has a notorious bar, and a consequent bore which runs as the tide comes in. Kingsley's poem about Mary who went to call the cattle home across the sands of the Dee, got caught in the mist which comes up with the fast-moving tide across the flats and 'never home came she' (or the cattle for that matter), is sadly true enough. The tide always comes in there so fast that it is fronted by at least a small wave, and no one but a fool would venture to race against the tide on foot. The Severn bore, predictable at certain tides, can be very impressive and goes miles up the river where it narrows, in the form of a breaking wave, until it eventually peters out against the force of water coming downstream.

SPRING AND NEAP TIDES

At fortnightly intervals, near enough, the sun and moon are in a straight line with the earth (at the time of full and new moon). The pull of the two together makes 'spring' tides when the tidal rise and fall is at its highest. The rest of the time the tidal range is less as the pull of the sun and moon conflict – this is the period of 'neap' tides. 'Spring' has nothing to do with that season. For gravitational reasons which can be calculated, some spring tides are likely to be bigger than others and this is noted on tide tables. Because the rise and fall of the tides must take place within the 12 hour and 25 minute period which is about half the time the moon takes to circle the earth, it follows that on spring tides the water will ebb and flow faster than it will at neap tides; there is more of it and it has to go further. This in turn affects the speed of the tidal streams, which are faster at spring tides and slower at neap tides. All this will affect the speed at which shallow areas of mud or sand flat become covered, and must be taken into account if you go out on to those areas.

From all this it follows that to live in safety by tidal waters you should make it your business to know about your local tides and their peculiarities, to find out how local weather conditions may affect them, and how they in turn affect the local weather (see Weather page 26). Use the tides, don't fight them.

Waves

Waves are made by the pressure of the wind which makes the sea rise and fall in a series of undulations. Strong winds make high waves, and the more open the sea the more room there is for huge waves to develop, tearing across the ocean. Inshore and in sheltered water the wind rarely forces the sea up into very big waves, but it can turn it into a dangerous seething 'chop' of short waves. The higher a wave becomes the less stable it is until it reaches a point where the face is not stable and must topple over forwards in foam. In deep water the movement of the particles as the wind blows on the surface is circular in a vertical plane, and each particle returns almost to its starting point on the surface, and the wave movement, the undulation, is transmitted forward so that the whole surface mass of water appears to move, which of course it does not until the waves reach shore. In shallow water there is just not room for the circular movement of the particles, so the wave towers up and becomes unstable, overbalances and breaks, and the whole mass of water it contains rushes forward up the beach. Waves upon rocky coasts break with enormous force as the wave movement through the water suddenly hits solid obstructions forcing the water to tower upwards in great bursts of spray, which may reach up to 300ft.

The power of tons of water suddenly releasing the wave energy it contains is fantastic and it is only when you have seen the damage to solid things that storm-driven seas can do that you really believe how powerful that millpond–calm summer sea can be.

Tidal Surges

A tidal surge is a phenomenon linked with tides and waves which can take place anywhere, but has with regularity plagued the eastern coast of England and the western coast of Holland. This is a North Sea surge, and nine have occurred this century. The worst was on the night of 31 January/1 February 1953, which flooded great areas in both countries and killed 307 people in this country alone. These surges are caused by combinations of unfortunate circumstances, north–easterly wind pushing extra water into the North Sea and a sudden drop of atmospheric pressure when it was already low, which allow the whole surface of the sea to rise above normal height, just as water sealed in a laboratory jar will rise if the atmospheric pressure inside is reduced by sucking out a little air. The North Sea down towards the Straits of Dover is a funnel and water forced into it must, at high tide, flood the land areas surrounding it. If a surge coincides with high spring tides then the flooding could be far worse than it was on that night in 1953 when the tides were not springs (see Floods page 155).

Tidal Ranges and Habitats

As described above the tidal range varies enormously according to whether it is spring or neap tides, or somewhere between, and according to the type of beach – shingle bank, shingle bank above sand, sand dunes and sand, rocky steep shore, or level estuary or saltmarsh. One section of any of these will be covered and exposed twice a day, that which lies between high and low water mark at neap tides, the smallest tidal range for that beach. Above that area the beach will only be covered twice a day as the tides approach springs, and below that area, the beach is only exposed twice a day as the tides approach springs, progressively more being covered or uncovered till spring tides are reached, and then progressively less as neaps approach. This obviously affects all plant and animal life and the beaches become divided into zones where the differing sets of circumstances encourage differing growths. In other words the habitats change radically over a very short distance. Starting just below dead low water springs there are the plants and animals which die if exposed to the air without a

Mussel beds and mudflats

covering of water, however shallow. Occasionally a combination of circumstances produces an extra low tide, exposing these plants and animals which cannot survive for long. Skin divers find that there is a very marked underwater line below which all kinds of plants and sea creatures thrive, and above which the shore is much more barren. On rocky shores there is often an area just below low tide level where the light and heat of the sun controls and affects the lives of the plants and animals that live in the shallow water. From above low water mark to high water mark live a succession of plants and animals which can tolerate the varying drying-out times, before the tide reaches them again. Some bury themselves in the wet sand and survive that way. Up at the top of the beach there are fewer and fewer marine plants and animals, and in fact it does become almost a desert especially where there is shingle. Water drains right down and out of the shingle, the stones grind together in the movement of the sea and nothing at all lives or grows. Then at the high water springs line, begin the land plants and animals; whereas the low tide dwellers are adapted to tolerate some fresh air and sunshine, the high water mark dwellers are adapted to tolerate limited amounts of saltiness and water, and in fact there is a whole range of plants which grow in estuaries and salt-marshes which live with their feet in salty mud and are frequently doused with salt spray or even submerged entirely. There are animals which live upon the surface of the mud, and another group living buried in it.

Marram grass and ragwort binding sand dunes

The effect of a North Sea surge

Above high water mark, sand dunes form yet another habitat, where marram grass stabilises and fertilises the sand and eventually sea spurge, sea holly and convolvulus and other plants colonise, and provide food for rabbits who burrow in the dunes and continue the process of turning sand to soil, progressively more capable of holding the moisture without which a plant cannot thrive.

Saltmarshes, formed at river mouths and in areas of wide estuaries inside spits and bars where continual silting up has gradually lifted them above high water mark, are a teeming habitat for all kinds of plants and animals. At high tide they are meadows of sea lavender, sea aster and marsh grass, with deep, main tidal channels and meandering shallow subsidiary channels and pools. As the tide falls, the water drains swiftly away leaving muddy flats and channels often quite deep in the middle where the outgoing tide scours them and it's almost impossible to cross on foot because the mud is soft, slippery and clinging, and flat meadows of marsh samphire, and small pools, lagoons and creeks.

Where there are rocky cliffs and rocky beaches, except for life in the rock pools, there is little life because the habitat is too battered by the sea, and the bases of the cliffs are also pretty bare. Higher up, though, where not quite so much water and spray lacerates the rock faces, and where seabirds have perched or nested and left guano in the crevices and on the ledges, yet two more types of plant colonise and hang on;

This North Sea surge deposited boats on to ornamental gardens

stonecrops and lichens. Only on the sheer chalk cliffs of southern England is there no life at all except for perching seabirds; yet even there where cliff falls have made sloping places, land plants have quickly colonised and rabbits and foxes abound.

So there is a succession of habitats and zones, some almost desert, others teeming with life, and the transition between the one and the other can cover just a few yards. Nowhere is there more life than in the mudflats and saltmarshes of estuaries, providing an endless food supply for seabirds and waders, and for man as well. Such places, where sea and country meet, do provide an excellent habitat for our species, especially as we alone have the capacity to build safe and (comparatively) indestructible shelters for ourselves, and to make and use boats and other artifacts.

Estuaries

The estuaries round our coasts vary in many ways. They have been forming over the centuries and very often today's wide estuary seems to bear little relation to the small river which empties through it. Once that river was a raging torrent carving its way to the sea loaded with silt in summer and churning ice in winter, and once the sea roared into the river mouth uninhibited by bars and sandbanks. Even now estuaries change continuously as yet more silt comes down the rivers, as sandbars and overfalls build up, or as water flow decreases because so much of it is taken for industrial or other human use. The building of reservoirs controlling river flow has reduced the scouring power of many rivers and in consequence estuaries silt up. In our own generation the pollution of rivers by chemical wastes has drastically altered the ecology of some estuaries, smothering the life in the previously rich and fertile estuary mud, which process eventually changes the look of the place and drives away the teeming population of seabirds and waders which once fed there.

In medieval times only those estuaries where water was always deep

A winter walk at the mouth of the Kentish Stour

The Shoreham Harbour dredger – antique but still at work

enough at high tide to float the little ships, where houses could be built near the water and horse transport brought alongside on wharves and jetties, developed as ports and harbours. Some still remain and have become complex modern ports, although constant dredging may be necessary to keep them deep enough for big ships. Such a harbour is Shoreham on the Sussex coast, where the river Adur enters the sea. For several centuries timber has been shipped in from the continent, and this trade, plus a great deal more, still continues. Other ports, once just as thriving, have died completely as the river mouths silted up and access to the wharves from the sea became impossible. Blakeney and Cley on the north Norfolk coast were once busy little ports, and so was Sandwich in Kent on the river Stour. Changes have taken place which have left other once busy seaside ports several miles from the water. Rye in Sussex can only take fishing boats these days, and is now several miles back from the sea which once came right up to it. Blakeney, Rye and Sandwich can all take yachts at high water, although the streams ebb to a shallow trickle.

Changes in the types of shipping and in the economics of transport have made such a difference. Where shallow-draught sailing barges by the score used the east coast estuaries and rivers to carry bricks, sand, coal, grain, shingle, all manner of cargoes which now go by lorry faster and more easily, only pleasure boats of all sizes, some of them those very same barges, now use the water; and if the rivers and estuaries become unnavigable except around high tides, it does not really matter for they are no longer seeking to deliver or collect cargoes on time.

Once the only houses and buildings near the water's edge, especially in the flat parts of our coastline where the winter wind blows very cold up the river mouths, were the homes of the fishermen and boatmen forced to live there, and their boatsheds and storehouses. Many of those buildings which survived are now the homes, or the holiday homes, of those who have moved away from towns and cities to the water's edge. More peaceful than the open sea coast and away from the noise of breaking waves, but nevertheless places where the views are wide and the skies enormous. Safe small-boat anchorages, and safe sailing water appeal to many. The naturalist goes for the birds and the fascinating botany of saltmarsh and sand dune. Estuaries in hill country, on the other hand, tend to be sheltered and not so wide, with hills backing the houses, and woods down to the water's edge. They are marvellous places to live in being sheltered from the open sea, yet with all the comings and goings of seafaring and estuary life right at hand.

The pressure of overpopulation in parts of this country sends people in their hundreds and thousands to the water's edge, mostly as holidaymakers, long or short term, but many do remain to live, and many others return again and again to the same place, where they can keep a boat, or have a small cottage or houseboat to live in some of the time. For these, estuary life is very different if they are new to it, from town life. There is always so much to do, so many varied things to look at and to learn.

Open Coastlines

The variety of coastal scenery round Britain is infinite and changes in comparatively short distances. What could be more different than the white cliffs of the Sussex coast and the shingle bank which runs eastwards from their ending at Beachy Head and Eastbourne, round Dungeness up to Deal. Or the sand dunes of Braunton Burrows and the headlands and long sandy beaches of Baggy Point and Croyde and Woolacombe just round the corner. Or the low sandy cliffs and fine sandy beaches of Sheringham, Cromer and Mundesley and the salt-

The White Cliffs of Dover: South Foreland lighthouses, old and new, and St Margaret's Bay windmill *(John Caughlin)*

marshes and sand dunes which run northwards from Salthouse to Brancaster.

All coastal towns are there for a reason; either they are at river mouths which have become resorts, or in sheltered coves where fishermen could safely keep their boats, and where during the last hundred years fine sands and good sea bathing have encouraged the holidaymaker until a big resort complete with promenades, piers, and amusement arcades has grown up, and hotels and boarding houses proliferate. There are still hundreds of miles of British coastline empty of people, except for those who deliberately seek out the lonely places. Exposed and dangerous coasts, coasts bounded by high and inaccessible cliffs, or cliffs and dunes swept in winter by bitter north-east winds where there is no shelter and no one would want to live. Living by the tidal waters of our open coast still has much in common with living by estuaries and tidal rivers, and so, is a part of this book, but there is no place here for the discussion of the merits of different resorts and beaches, or the availability of camp sites. That can all be found in books which cater specifically for that kind of thing.

FURTHER READING Smith, A. and Southam, J. *Good Beach Guide* (Penguin); Yonge, C. M. *The Sea Shore* (Fontana); Carson, Rachel. *The Sea Around Us* (Panther); Evans, I. O. *The Observer's Book of Sea and Sea Shore* (Warne); Soper, Tony. *The Shell Book of Beachcombing* (David & Charles).

2

Weather

Much money and time and effort are expended on weather forecasting, and the computerised data and photographs from satellites, weather ships and countless shore stations still fail with regularity to forecast our weather, especially in local and detailed terms. Scattered thunderstorms turn out to be vicious electrical storms of tropical intensity; moderate Force 4 to 5 winds become howling gales, and rain in the afternoon arrives during the morning. Yet it is possible, by using basic meteorological equipment, your powers of observation and some local knowledge, to predict short-term local weather with some accuracy.

The anticyclonic systems, which bring fine weather, the troughs and ridges which separate them from the depressions which bring our bad weather, commonly move from west to east across the British Isles. In bad weather, stand with your back to the wind, and the centre of the cyclone or depression will be away to your left, and probably travelling in an easterly or slightly north-easterly direction. This will give you some idea of how long it will be before the bad weather passes. The anticyclone or high pressure system tends to build up and remain much more static than the cyclone, and gives rise to long periods of fine weather before it gives way to the pressures of approaching cyclones and the troughs and fronts which precede them.

Coastal and estuary weather, specially in terms of rainfall, snowfall, frost and fog may be quite different from that just a couple of miles inland, or out at sea.

The barometer, which measures atmospheric pressure, is the one vital piece of equipment, and although it cannot predict wind direction or forces, it does indicate change, and the type of change, and used in conjunction with other information and observation, pretty good predictions can be made. The barometric pressure is higher for

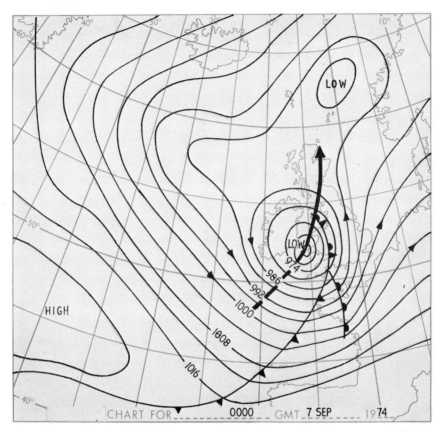

CHART FOR ...... 0000 ... GMT 7 SEP 19 74

Deep depression in the Irish Sea moving northeast: after the summer lull, the reappearance of disturbed weather often occurs in September – the well known autumnal gales. This is a good example. Gales, probably severe, already occurring in the southwest approaches, the Channel, and Biscay, will rapidly spread to the North Sea as the deepening depression moves northeast and turns to the left towards the Moray Firth. The gales will be particularly severe as the wind funnels through the Straits of Dover.

To the west of the British Isles, unstable polar air will bring squally showers to many areas with possibly more general rain as the trough of low pressure to the northwest of Ireland swings southeast behind the depression

easterly and northerly winds than for westerly and southerly winds. North-easterly winds raise the glass most, south-westerlies depress it most. Usually the glass falls for a southerly and rises for a northerly, but should it do the opposite, and rise although the wind remains southerly, then it is unlikely to rain, but a fall with a northerly wind indicates strong winds and rain or snow. High pressure means good weather, low pressure means bad weather. If the glass rises rapidly

Light fine weather cumulus

then a quick change for the better is on the way, but it may be short lived. If it rises slowly but steadily then the weather will improve slowly but may hold.

A falling glass in summer, below seasonal levels (higher in summer), means high wind and rain. Test the air temperature and if it is warm and feels damp, the high wind will be southerly with rain; if it is cold it will be northerly with less rain. A barometer unseasonably low which begins to rise, predicts a wind shift to northerly, sometimes with strong squalls and showers. In winter a suddenly falling glass and a drop in temperature means snow.

During settled weather in this country the wind may veer round (clockwise) during the day, following the sun, and then go back at evening to its original direction. If the wind moves definitely anti-clockwise against the sun, say from north-west to south-west then there is bad weather coming.

Settled fine weather round our islands is characterised by northerly or north-westerly winds and light high mackerel clouds to begin with. As the high pressure system stabilises the clouds become lower and fleecier, especially in the afternoon. In early morning there will be a mist near the water's edge and just out to sea which will dissolve as the sun gets higher. Breezes blowing onshore develop during the day but never become very strong, and drop right away towards evening and perhaps become offshore after dark. A typical sea-breeze day has bright blue skies early on and light cumulus clouds develop. In the morning gentle winds blow offshore and the warm air rises. The gentle but colder sea breeze begins to blow onshore and forms a small front, characterised by a line of light cloud along the shore or just inland, literally dividing the sky in half, with cloudless blue sky over the sea and light cumulus clouds blowing from the land to the coast and disappearing right over the shoreline. Along the actual front line over the water's edge there can be quite dramatic wind shifts as one or other of the breezes becomes dominant. If such a day starts with onshore winds, then the sea breeze will be quite strong by the middle of the day. During the evenings of sea-breeze days, the wind dies away and blows lightly offshore. Such sea breezes are more common on east- and south-facing coasts, especially where the land is low by the shore with low hills inland.

The line of cloud which forms along shorelines on sea-breeze days can be a useful guide, if you have sailed out to sea, as to where the land lies. These clouds form over islands as well and are sure indication of land below even when it cannot be seen. The Maori name for New Zealand is 'Land of the Long White Cloud' for there is always cloud over the warm land in the cool southern sea.

In fine weather the glass rises very slowly and steadily and there will be heavy dewfall every night. When the glass stops rising and there is no dew then the following day the sky is a harder blue and not so soft and hazy and the wind backs southerly as the barometric pressure falls. High up there are mares-tails, followed by lower darkish clouds; the glass continues to fall and the sky becomes overcast, heavy and damp, and the rain arrives perhaps with widespread and diffuse thunder and lightning.

These frontal storms are quite different in character from the heavy storms from enormous towering cumulus clouds which build up in hot humid weather, and produce prodigious and terrifying lightning and heavy hail and rain, such as the tempests of north Norfolk which usually advance from the north-west, and occasionally from the

Island cloud

south-east. The same type of heavy storms advance from France heading across the Channel to beat upon south-east England. In fine weather the lower level of air is stable and little cloud develops, but it eventually becomes so warm that it breaks through the inversion or layer of cold air which is holding it down and cumulo–nimbus grows in the unstable air above to produce these storms. Thunderstorms have extremely local habits, however, and thunder-squalls frequently follow a line of hills and ignore the lower valleys between. The worst of the storms coming down the Thames estuary run along the northern Kent coast and out to sea, leaving untouched the low ground between the Isle of Thanet and the chalk ridge of the North Downs which ends at Dover. Other storms may at the same time come right down that ridge of Downs and out to sea. So it certainly pays to watch the tracks of thunderstorms in your area and while of course there are no hard and fast rules, some places certainly get it much worse than others.

Under certain atmospheric conditions mist and fog persist in river valleys, estuaries and shorelines. Particularly in spring and autumn, exceptionally hot days followed by a cold wind off the sea, may produce a shallow belt of heavy coastal fog caused by the moisture in the air condensing as it is chilled over the sea. This fog is immediately evaporated again just a few hundred yards inland as the warm earth reheats the air, and the sun shines bright and hot. This same phenomenon of mist coming up with the tide in estuaries is caused by cold advancing sea chilling the moisture-laden air and condensation taking place. This condensation is the formation of dew and the temperature at which it happens is known as 'dewpoint' and these fogs are really ground-level clouds. Fog persists in valleys where a cold layer of air is trapped under a warm layer, and low mist forms. There is usually little wind associated with mist or fog, except for the sea mist described above, but mist and strong wind always mean rain to follow. Dew and ground mists will not form in windy weather as wind prevents the air from cooling to dewpoint. Neither does dew form in cloudy weather as the clouds prevent the warmth of the day dissipating by radiation and the ground-level air remains too warm to form dew.

Clouds

I have already mentioned the flying mares-tails of high cirrus cloud which precede a rainy front. If these are pointing upwards the rain will follow very soon, but if they are scattered across the sky the rain will

Storm sky, Isle of Thanet, North Kent coast

still come but not quite so soon. The wind will veer in the direction in which the clouds cross the sky, but if the ends of the wisps are turning back, then the wind will eventually change to that direction.

Cumulus clouds rise up in light bulbous masses from flat bases; small cumulus clouds in rows or banks move across fine-weather afternoon skies and die away towards sunset in stable fine weather. Heavy cumulo-nimbus clouds which tower upwards and upwards from dark bases until high up they spread out into anvil-shaped clouds, mean at best heavy showers and some thunder, at worst very bad thunderstorms, usually easing off by evening.

Between the very high-level cirrus clouds and the cumulus clouds is the cirro-stratus, thin hazy cloud which forms haloes round the sun or moon, and may mean approaching rain. Below this the cirro-cumulus clouds form a true mackerel sky which looks like ripples on a low tide sand. This usually means an unsettled day, but with not too much rain. Alto-stratus also forms a haziness in the sky giving rise to sun and moon haloes, but is lower than the cirrus clouds. Cumulus clouds in various forms are the most common clouds. There are the globular alto-cumulus, the cumulus-castellatus which forms middle-height individual turret-shaped clouds, and mammato-cumulus which hangs in little inverted globules beneath black storm clouds and indicates a lot of turbulence.

The stratus clouds, as apart from alto-stratus, are the rain clouds which form at various levels. Strato-cumulus is a layer or patches of globular clouds, soft and grey and more or less in lines. The ragged layer of low-level rain cloud, grey and formless, is nimbo-stratus. When this is very ragged and windblown, with broken high clouds above it, the rain will be very heavy.

In deteriorating summer weather, line-squalls may form. These are comparatively narrow bands of heavy swirling cumulo-nimbus cloud stretching back upwind for up to several miles. Usually there is a lighter grey, slightly lower cloud just ahead of the main cloud, formed by the down-draught of wind that always precedes these squalls. If this sudden wind arrives, lifting the dust and rattling the trees, then the squall is coming straight at you, and it is best to find shelter. The storm squall will arrive with more wind, rain and thunder, and be violent as long as it lasts. If you are off to one side of it, then winds may be unpredictable as they rush in to the turbulence of the squall, and this kind of storm frequently capsizes dinghies and creates locally very bad conditions for a short while. Strong and dangerous gusts of wind are associated with line-squalls. Each side of the squall the sky may be perfectly clear and the sun shining.

While a coppery sky high up in heavy cloud may be very threatening, if the coppery look is low down, just above ground level, behind

Typical anvil cloud building up

Ragged rain cloud

the greyness of an approaching bank of cloud, then that just means that beyond the cloud the sun is shining, and the skies will soon clear again, if only temporarily.

Wind and storms quite a long way off start wave movements in the sea, and a swell on a calm day for no apparent local reason may mean that a storm is on the way, especially if it is coming from the same direction as the wind. The movement of layers of cloud in different directions one above the other is a sign of disturbance and possible storms and wind shifts before long. Clouds moving in a different direction from that of the ground wind, also indicate disturbed weather, which when it arrives will bring an instant and dramatic change in the direction of the ground wind.

If you are actually on the water, especially in a sailing boat, literally keep a weather eye open; advancing puffs of wind and squalls always darken the water to windward, and you can be ready for the cat's-paw or gust when it reaches you. On days of patchy fast-moving cloud there may be stronger wind beneath the clouds than in the clear sunlit patches. If the wind becomes fitful and dies away to nothing, and the water goes 'clock' calm, watch out for wind shifts. Keep looking all around and if you see a dark line on the water at the horizon, watch it, as it may well be a wind shift advancing upon you. The first puff of a wind shift is always quite strong and fierce for a few moments, but shortly drops back to a steady wind speed. Only in obviously thundery weather, when fierce wind shifts can occur at any time, are such winds dangerous. If you are ready for them, then they should cause no trouble.

If you happen to live on our westerly coasts facing the prevailing south-westerly winds, then rainfall will not be so heavy as it is a few miles inland. The warm wet west winds do not drop their load until they have reached the shore and been lifted up by the wind to cross the cliffs and hills. By the same reasoning, these clouds having crossed, for instance, the Cornwall/Devon peninsula, do not have so much rain left to drop along the south coast, so rainfall is less. This applies to any place in the rain shadow of high country. The Moray Firth on the east coast of Scotland enjoys better weather and lower rainfall than do the Great Glen and the Highlands to the west.

Weather Portents

Local phenomena such as a hill where mist always forms and rolls downwards before rain, or a lot of woodland near the sea which encourages mist in certain conditions, may also help you to forecast local weather, but so far no mention has been made of weather lore usually in the form of rhymes, and the clues which can be gained from the behaviour of living things. Wild yellow or red skies at sunset or sunrise usually mean rain on the way, and only the bright and then dull red hazy glow of a fine summer sunset is the 'red sky at night, sailors' delight'. The yellower and thinner the sunset, the nearer the rain. The harsher and harder the blue of the sky, the nearer the rain. The sharper the coastal visibility, the nearer the rain.

Coastal areas are warmer at night than inland at all times of the year, especially in late spring and early autumn. Although I have seen the sea's edge frozen in south-eastern England, frosts are not usually too hard near the sea, and hoar frost caused by freezing mist making crystals on plants is rare by the water's edge. Hard frost may still clamp down in fine settled winter weather. If the frost disappears quickly, then a change is on the way to slightly warmer and wetter, windier weather, and the glass will be falling. Frost is usually associated with high barometric pressure, as is dew in summertime.

Our rheumatic bones ache as the pressure drops and bad weather approaches. Tempers get short in hot thundery weather, heads ache and there is a feeling of fear or excitement as storms come near. We

Forerunner of a line squall

seek shelter from wind and rain. All animals, birds and insects react to the weather, and so do many plants, and it is by observation of their behaviour, usually more acute and timely than our own, that the most accurate forecasting can be done. On a winter day when the gulls fly inland in ragged groups in their hundreds, then a gale and bad weather is surely not far behind. In summer pheasants 'clock' in alarm at distant thunder which they hear long before we do, and bees pouring back to their hives and homes are a sure sign that a storm is on its way. Bees hate thunderstorms and lightning and never get caught out in the rain. Many insects hatch in humid weather, and martins and other insec-tivorous birds flying low over grass and water are taking the insects as they hatch. Storms may follow humid weather. Other insects have mating flights, much higher up in fine weather, or hatch and migrate in great clouds. High-flying martins, swifts and swallows take harvest of this and so this is a sign of good weather. Warble-flies like to lay their eggs in the legs of cattle in humid weather so the sight of cattle running with their tails raised, to escape the noisy warble-flies, indicates that storms may arrive soon. Most animals are restless before approaching storms: pigs squeal noisily, and cockerels crow. If the birds fall silent during hot weather it usually means that thunder is coming, and rooks will not leave their nests before a storm. Screech owls are noisier before rain.

Watch for unusual behaviour in your domestic animals. Dogs and cats are so humanised as not to react at all in a characteristic way. One cat may rush about with 'the wind in its tail' before gales, another may curl up with its tail across its face to sleep out the storm. Some dogs are terrified by approaching thunderstorms which they sense before you do. Others take no notice at all.

All freshwater fishermen know that insects hatch under certain fine weather conditions, and that this brings fish up, and birds down to feed. Pike tend to remain quietly on the stream bed when rain or wind or cold weather are on the way, and trout do not take the fly so readily when there are storms about. When freshwater clams release plenty of air bubbles, rain is imminent; and frogs croak loudly before wet weather. Plants can be good weather forecasters. The little scarlet pimpernel, a common weed in short grassland and cornfields, closes its petals when rain is on the way or when the air is humid, and only opens up in hot dry sunshine. The famous piece of seaweed, hung outside the door as a rain predictor, is quite accurate. The leathery, salty flesh desiccates and shrivels in dry hot air, but the salt immediately absorbs any atmospheric moisture and the seaweed becomes a little more supple again. It is the hygroscopic salt which is really

Bad weather sunset – gales and rain likely

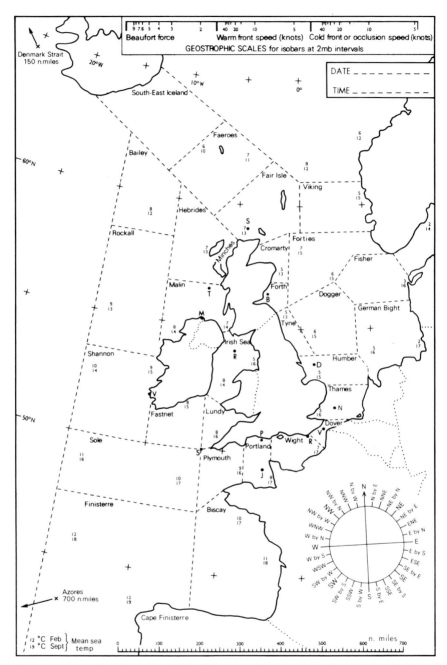

Sea areas as referred to in BBC Shipping Forecasts (as shown on R. Met. Soc./R.Y.A. Metmap for yachtsmen)

indicating approaching and present humidity. If the seaweed is left where rain washes it, the salt will eventually leach out and it won't work any more, so hang your piece of kelp or seawrack somewhere where it will not get wet. Dandelions close before storms, pondweed sinks before rain. The leaves of many broad-leaved trees, sycamores, limes and plane trees, turn up their undersides before storms.

Local weather forecasts for all coastal areas can be obtained by telephone. Look in your local code directory. These forecasts are issued at various regular times during the day and recorded, and a dialled call connects you to the tape recorder. These forecasts are usually to be relied upon, but even so can be subject to local variation. The coastguards will impart weather information if you ring them, but not in too much detail. They will certainly tell you present temperatures, wind speeds, type of weather, etc. Local RAF stations may also oblige. Look up the number of the station in your phone book and ask for the Met Office. You won't get a flea in your ear from either of these sources, for people naturally like to be consulted, and to feel that their expertise is used and appreciated.

For the purposes of weather forecasting, Great Britain and its surrounding sea areas are divided into sections, and shipping forecasts (see *Radio Times*) continually refer to these. If you are interested in keeping weather records, contact the Meteorological Office who will help you with forms, etc, and if you are prepared to take rain-gauge readings, temperature readings, etc, etc, 365 days a year, may in certain areas be glad of your information.

Making a Weather Vane

If you are a handyman you can make a strong weather vane to any design you like, without welding. (This is not recommended for beginners though.) First think exactly where and how you will mount it. To fix it to a chimney or gable-end requires rigid bracketing and anchoring for a weather vane is heavy and its movement puts great strain on its fixings.

You will need: enough 22 or 16 gauge mild steel sheeting for the vane panel, bracer bar and cardinal points bar; 2ft of $\frac{1}{2} \times \frac{1}{4}$in mild steel strip to weight the pointer end; 5in of mild steel tube big enough to slip over a $\frac{1}{2}$in phosphor bronze bearing 1in long (from an agricultural engineer); a length of $\frac{1}{2}$in mild steel rod on which to pivot and mount the vane; some $\frac{1}{8}$in rivets; 1 bolt $1 \times \frac{1}{4}$in; a tube of Plastic Padding. A blacksmith will sell you the steel or tell you where it can be obtained.

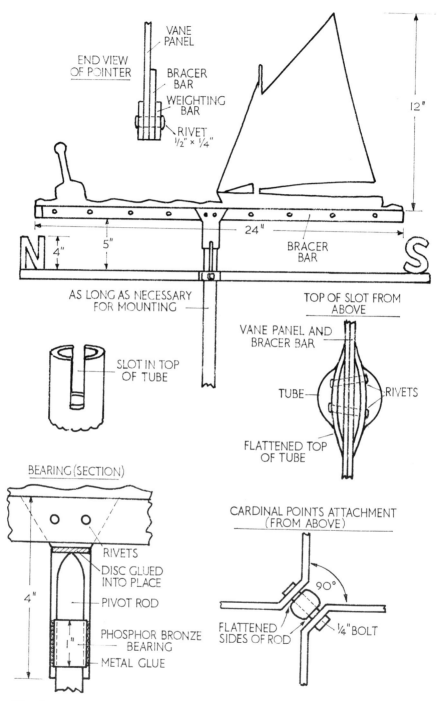

END VIEW OF POINTER

VANE PANEL

BRACER BAR

WEIGHTING BAR

RIVET 1/2" × 1/4"

12"

24"

BRACER BAR

N

S

4"

5"

AS LONG AS NECESSARY FOR MOUNTING

SLOT IN TOP OF TUBE

TOP OF SLOT FROM ABOVE

VANE PANEL AND BRACER BAR

TUBE

RIVETS

FLATTENED TOP OF TUBE

BEARING (SECTION)

RIVETS

DISC GLUED INTO PLACE

PIVOT ROD

PHOSPHOR BRONZE BEARING

METAL GLUE

4"

1"

CARDINAL POINTS ATTACHMENT (FROM ABOVE)

90°

FLATTENED SIDES OF ROD

1/4" BOLT

Weather vane

Tools: a coping saw, a drill with $\frac{1}{4}$in and $\frac{1}{8}$in bits, a hammer and a file, a centre punch.

These materials will make a vane with an overall length of 24in with a wind panel no bigger than 12in square. Bigger vanes require heavier rod, tube and bearings.

A weather vane works because the windage on one side of the pivot is greater than on the other, so whatever your design the widest part must be on one side. The pivot point should be as near the centre of the vane panel as possible while still achieving this. Weight must be nearly equal on each side of the pivot, or the vane will not turn and it will put an uneven strain on its wall mounting as it tries to sag towards its heaviest side. It is usually necessary to add bars or a lump of metal at the pointer end to even up the weight.

Draw your design full size on paper, cut it out and stick it to the sheet metal. Cut it out with the coping saw. Cut another strip for the bracing bar 1in wide and rivet it along the bottom of the panel, having drilled matching holes in both pieces. Suspend this on a piece of string at about the point where it will pivot. Cut the $\frac{1}{2} \times \frac{1}{4}$in weighting strip in half and lodge or hang the pieces on the pointer end, then cut pieces down until you have achieved as good a weight balance as possible. Sandwich the pointer ends between the two weighting strips, riveting or sticking them into place. (They can be soldered if you know how to solder.)

Cut a slot 1in deep in the top of the tube, exactly the width of the bottom of the panel and bracer bar. Cut a disc of sheeting which will fit tightly into the tube, lay it flat and using a centre punch make a deep mark exactly in the middle of it. Fit this disc into the tube, mark down, and tap it down to $\frac{1}{2}$in below the slot. Put a ribbon of Plastic Padding right round both sides of it to stick it to the tube. Fit the vane panel into the slot, hammer the tube flat each side of it and rivet the whole thing right through with two rivets. Stick the phosphor bronze bearing just inside the lower end of the tube with Plastic Padding. File the top of the pivot rod to a point which will fit into the punch mark in the disc and slide it up inside the tube. It must turn absolutely freely. If it does not, file it down until it does.

Cut the two cardinal points pieces out of sheeting and bend them to the shape shown, by hammering them over the edge of a vice. Fit them as shown on to the rod just enough below the tube for the letters to clear the vane panel. Flatten the two opposite sides of the rod with a file, drilling a $\frac{1}{4}$in hole through both pieces and the rod. Do up the bolt as tightly as you possibly can.

Paint the whole thing with metal primer, and then with black polyurethane metal paint, and mount it securely in its final position. Use a compass to be sure you have set it to magnetic north, then turn the whole contraption 8° clockwise to true north, before finally bolting it tight. Wait for a Force 3 (or more) wind, which is what any vane needs to register properly, before you condemn it as useless.

FURTHER READING The Meteorological Office. *Elementary Meteorology* (HMSO); Holford, Ingrid. *Interpreting The Weather* (David & Charles); Watts, Alan. *Instant Wind Forecasting* (Peter Davies); Watts, Alan. *Instant Weather Forecasting* (Peter Davies); Miller, Austin and Parry, M. *Everyday Meteorology* (Hutchinson); Bowen, D. *Britain's Weather* (David & Charles); Lester, N. M. *The Observer's Book of the Weather* (Warne).

USEFUL ADDRESS *The Meteorological Office,* Met 08B, London Road, Bracknell, Berks; 26 Palmerston Place, Edinburgh 12.

3

Coastal Services

Coastguards

Originally concerned only with customs and excise, through the centuries the revenue men fought a continuous war against the smugglers around our south-east coasts; a war which frequently erupted into bloody battles, and which had a full intelligence service of spies and informers. The officers were usually at a disadvantage because the local populace at all levels hated paying the high taxes which smuggled goods did not carry.

The prevention of smuggling, including that of human beings, into this country, is still part of the coastguards' job, but gradually over the years the service has become more and more concerned with safety at sea and with the control of shipping in congested sea-lanes such as the Straits of Dover. From the lonely cliff-top hut of fifty years ago, equipped with binoculars or telescope, telephone and sometimes with a not very efficient radio, to the highly sophisticated mass of electronic equipment, radio and radar, which is the modern station at South Foreland, is a far cry. However, right round our coasts are coastguard stations big and small according to the needs of the area, all manned by trained full-time and part-time men (and women). The coastguards are also trained in the use of the rescue equipment carried in the station Land Rover – breeches-buoy gear which can still be the only way to get people ashore on rocky coasts, tackle for lowering men down cliffs to rescue the stranded (and that can be hair raising however well you are trained) – and in working with both lifeboat and helicopter crews when necessary. The coastguard is the co-ordinator of first-phase air-sea rescue work, and it is he who in response to calls for help by telephone, radio or flare, alerts the appropriate services. In some areas coastguards badly need auxiliary help in manning stations at peak times, and should you be interested, go along to the station where the chief officer will give you full information about training etc.

Coastguards keep full weather records, nowadays mostly gathered electronically, and are part of the set-up providing information for the Meteorological Office. Should you wish for local weather information, try the coastguards; they are unfailingly helpful, and anything that worries you or seems unusual on the sea or on the beach should be reported to them. They can be reached in an emergency via a 999 call. They will want to know all the details you have of your problem, whether it is a boat or a person in trouble, particularly position. You are not expected to give compass bearings, but should give a rough idea in relation to something on shore – a wood, a church, a house, a breakwater. The coastguards will take all necessary action. If it all turns out to be nothing, they do not mind in the least. It is far better to report trouble even if you are not quite sure if it is trouble or not. Speed is usually desperately important in life saving so never waste time wondering what to do. Act.

Air-Sea Rescue

Based at strategic points round our coasts are the yellow RAF helicopters of the Air-Sea Rescue Service. Working closely with the coastguards and lifeboat services they have already saved hundreds of lives, and at the same time are training service personnel in helicopter rescue work. Do not try to call them directly, report to the coastguards and leave it to them. Helicopters may not go more than 5 miles out to sea without an escort, usually provided by a lifeboat.

Lifeboats

The astonishing thing about our Royal National Lifeboat Institution is that its boats are all manned by volunteer crews. The key men, coxswains (the coxswain is the boss), the second coxswain and mechanic, do receive a regular small payment and a 'reward' is paid to crew members for every service they do, to compensate for loss of earnings. They and those who man the fast inshore-rescue boats which have lately become a vital part of the service, are of course highly trained. Traditionally, the local longshoremen and those whose livelihoods were directly concerned with the sea manned the boats, but nowadays, especially as longshore fishing has drastically declined, men from all walks of life are included in the crew, provided they are trained.

44

RAF rescue helicopter *(RAF Manston)*

Its lifeboat is a source of great pride to every town or area where one of the 138 boats are stationed, and competition for a crew place can be fierce. When the maroons sound, two unmistakable explosions like nothing else (in peacetime), the crewmen drop everything (I have even seen an abandoned milk float) and race to the lifeboat station. The coxswain takes his crew from the first comers. There is a list of acceptable men, and for instance, at Walmer, where the boat takes a crew of seven, the first three belts go to the coxswain, his second and the engineer, the other four are taken by the first comers. This boat is usually afloat, even at low water when a long row of huge timber planks must be laid down the beach to make a slipway, within six minutes of the maroons sounding.

Often the boat is water-borne before the crew are told by radio exactly what it is they are looking for.

Salvage laws are complex, but occasionally the crew picks up a good bonus of salvage money. Much more often nowadays, they rescue those whose foolishness one way or another has landed them in trouble. Those who, like the jumblies, went to sea in a sieve, or without knowing the rudiments of navigation. Recently an old unseaworthy yacht went ashore on the Goodwins. The lifeboat, without whose help the boat must have been lost and the crew drowned, arrived, and one of its crew boarded the yacht.

'You will use *my* tow rope,' said the yacht owner. 'I know the laws of salvage.'

'You know . . . all,' replied the lifeboatman. 'And what do you take us for?'

That same lifeboatman very nearly lost his life last year when he became trapped by the legs, having gone through the deck of a sinking yacht which the lifeboat was trying to tow to harbour. Another lifeboatman, with enormous effort, pulled him clean out of his boots just as the yacht sank. Both men were picked up semi-conscious with effort and shock, half drowned and kept afloat by their lifejackets, by the rest of the lifeboat crew. All in an attempt to save the property of a complete stranger.

'It seemed a pity to let it sink, it was a nice boat and it wasn't really their fault things had gone wrong,' said the man who nearly drowned.

The RNLI has saved getting on for 100,000 lives and costs at least £2 million a year to run, all gathered by voluntary subscription.

Lighthouses

Not, I suppose, strictly to do with living by the sea, except for lighthouse keepers, but they are such splendid and important features of coastal landscape that they must have a mention. There are half a dozen remains of towers round our coasts which are believed to be Roman lighthouses, but pride of place goes to the pharos at Dover, marking the cliffs above the Roman settlement there, for the guidance of ships coming across from Boulogne (where there was another such tower). It is a flint and tile course tower, on the top floor of which a beacon fire would be lit. Now it stands as the most ancient lighthouse building in Britain. A couple of miles north, right on the corner of England on the high white cliffs, stands the South Foreland light-house. Nearby, right on the cliff edge, is the old lighthouse, the first to have electricity to power its light, which could be seen for 27 miles.

Moving south to the great triangular shingle spit of Dungeness, the old lighthouse and its keepers' homes still stand in front of the nuclear

The Roman pharos, Dover   South Foreland lighthouse

power station, and like many coastal lighthouses can be visited and climbed if you have the stomach for heights. It has been superseded by the most modern automatic lighthouse in Britain, built in 1966, just a few hundred yards away, with a 4 million candle-power light. Made of huge concrete rings one upon the other, it is a mass of electronic light and sound equipment, and at the same time manages to be extremely elegant.

Below Beachy Head is perhaps the closest inshore of our sea-girt lighthouses, 'Belle Toute'; this was one of the last towers to be built of interlocking granite blocks. Sea-girt towers withstand pressures up to

(*Above*) Belle Toute – Beachy
Head lighthouse
(*Below*) The new Dungeness
lighthouse

6,000lb per square foot. Beachy Head light is 153ft high, but dwarfed by the 536ft chalk cliffs around. All the materials were carried to it down a cableway from the top of the cliff. Way out to sea round our coast are other lonely granite towers marking dangerous rocks and reefs; Eddystone is probably the most famous of these, Wolf Rock and Bishop's Rock being two more which get into the news when continuous storms create such huge seas that relief of the keepers becomes impossible for weeks on end. A BBC man went to Bishop's Rock for a three-day Christmas broadcast and finally got home a month later! Lighthouse keeping was always a lonely job, and still is in those offshore towers, but modern communications and motor cars mean that even the remotest coastal lights are no longer quite so cut off. Yet for wives and families in some it can still be a lonely job; lighthouses are not often in the middle of a village or on the edge of the town as is, for instance, North Foreland, which also houses a very important radio-telephone system for ship-to-shore communication. Hartland lighthouse, on Hartland Point, with its cluster of keepers' houses is shorebased, but still very isolated. Longstones, the tower lighthouse on the Farne Islands off the Northumberland coast, once the home of the keeper William Darling and his famous daughter Grace, is in a sense land based, but is miles from anywhere.

At the age of five I was very impressed with the view from the top of St Mary's lighthouse at the north end of Whitley Bay. There is a cluster of houses on an islet, joined to the shore by a causeway. Once there was a chapel, an ale house, and even a graveyard for shipwrecked mariners. The traditions of the ale house were maintained in so far as I was bought a bottle of cherryade to refresh me after the climb up and down!

If you live in view of a lighthouse, the rhythmic sweep of the beam at night will light your room, and you will need quite thick curtains to keep it out, for the light is designed to carry up to 30 miles or so. The lamp room may be screened on the landward side to cut down the amount of light uselessly illuminating the countryside. Of course the carry of the beam is affected by the height of the tower above sea level. Towers on sea rocks, or low cliffs or at beach level are as high as they can conveniently be built, but lighthouses on headlands, already hundreds of feet above sea level, need be no higher than is sufficient to clear surrounding or neighbouring buildings.

Although the tall tower of Calais lighthouse is 30 miles from where I live, and below the horizon, I can on clear nights see the loom of the light as it turns, rather like a distant searchlight.

The modern automatic lighthouse does have a keeper, but he has a system of coded signals and messages with which he can control the various mechanisms from a distance. The lighthouse also has a series of vocal recordings and other signals. The keeper can literally ask the lighthouse to report to him by means of these recordings, and the coded signals will immediately alert him in case of any mechanical faults. Therefore he can live some miles from the light if necessary.

Lighthouses are run by Trinity House which probably originated in the thirteenth century and collects dues from shipping using the seas and harbours round our coasts to pay for the upkeep of the lights.

Lightships

A CHRISTMAS TRIP TO THE LIGHTSHIPS

Nine miles long and up to a mile wide, the Goodwin Sands, the 'Shippe Swallower', lie off the Kent coast in the northern exit of the Straits of Dover, right on the short route from the Channel to the mouth of the Thames. They still take their toll with deadly regularity in spite of radar. Now they are marked by three lightships, many channel buoys and two lighthouses.

All I could see from the deck of the Ramsgate lifeboat was water and sandbank, innocuous enough for the sea was flat calm and I could have waded ashore and walked among the gullies and humps, putting up flights of greater black-backed gulls – the corpse eaters as the seamen call them – that haunt this sinister place. In half an hour when the tide begins to flow those firm sands become quicksands on which a man must run flat out to stay on top. In there somewhere under the sand lies what is left of the old South Goodwin lightship. Twenty years ago in a storm she broke her huge mooring cable and drifted north on the tide from her station down at the other end of the sands. Helpless, for lightships have no motive power, she went on the sands hereabouts and was lost with all hands but one, a bird watcher who was rescued by RAF Air-Sea Rescue helicopter.

Our present errand was very different and the unnautical collection of people on the boat included Father Christmas in full rig, the Mayor of Ramsgate with his chain of office over a duffel coat, and a few seasick choirboys in surplices. We were on the Christmas run to the North and East Goodwin Light Vessels. We left Ramsgate harbour early on a wet morning, loaded with two huge turkeys, sacks of potatoes, bags of mail, two Christmas trees and several hundred-weight of Christmas food and drink for the crews of the two light-

50

The Mayor of Ramsgate on a Christmas visit to a lightship

ships, from well-wishers including the local boat clubs. First we went to the North Goodwin, put there to warn ships off the North Sand Head. The first lightship went on station here in 1795. She was an old converted merchantman and manning her must have been hell in those days long before radar, radio, electric light, foghorns, refrigerators and tinned food. The crew banged a gong when it was foggy, and the lantern was dim, but it was better than nothing. If they saw a ship heading for trouble they fired rockets to warn them, and a cannon to alert the fishermen at Deal and Ramsgate, who put off in their luggers and saved many a life from the sands, and lost many a life in so doing. That was before the days of the RNLI.

The North Goodwin Light Vessel is painted brave red with her name in big white letters on the side. She looks very small beside a supertanker. We went alongside and, led by Father Christmas, all climbed aboard. The boxes of food were carefully handed up for it would have been a real tragedy to drop one into the sea, especially as we had been lucky enough to have a calm delivery day. We went aft for the ceremony of hauling the tree to the truck of the mast. We sang 'Oh God our help in ages past' and 'Oh come all ye faithful' to the sky and the sea. We took a quick look round the ship, including the galley with its big old iron stove pushing out waves of heat, and its ever-boiling kettle. The 'on-duty' crew comprises six men and a master, and they take it in turns to cook. It struck me that the stove would be red hot for the next ten days or so. The full crew is eleven, two masters and nine men. The masters relieve each other once a month, while the men do a month on ship and a fortnight on shore. Four out of five lightshipmen are married; the single ones don't stick it very long. The ship is draughty when she pitches in a running sea and

The North Goodwin lightship: the galley

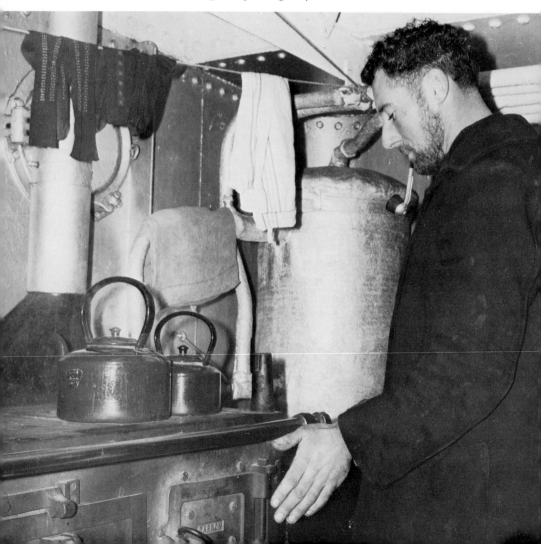

the motion squeezes air up through the decks. Apparently one gets used to the foghorn.

After we returned to the lifeboat, the lightship let off a couple of blasts which nearly lifted us off the deck. The foghorn is a rubber diaphragm which is vibrated by a blast of compressed air. When the air is shut off the diaphragm deafeningly slams back on to its seating.

An hour later we reached the East Goodwin on her station halfway down the outside of the sands. She too came off her mooring in a gale a few years ago. She drifted 2 miles before the crew even realised she was away. There is nothing to take bearings on out there on a dark stormy night. They dropped their spare anchor in time, before she went on the sands like her sister ship the South Goodwin, so that incident had a happy ending.

As we left, a coaster motoring by dipped her own masthead tree in Christmas greeting and again we suffered the blasting of that violent foghorn. Only at Christmas does anyone except the relief tender pay a call, though several thousand ships a year pass safely by.

Channel Buoys and Charts

All lighthouses and lightships flash their lights and sound their foghorns or signals at regular and consistent intervals, clearly stated on Admiralty charts. The Admiralty chart for your area is essential if you wish to go to sea with any degree of safety, except perhaps for very local sailing or fishing.

As well as detailing buoys, lights, etc, Admiralty charts show very clearly the limits of sandbanks, channels and depths by means of numbers all over each chart. These numbers indicate the mean level of low water spring tides. In other words the shallowest it should ever be excepting in very unusual circumstances. Tidal information and tidal flow directions are clearly shown. Admiralty charts are available for various harbours and for coastal areas as well as for deep-sea passages. Other firms publish charts which show detailed harbour and tidal information. Ask at a good yachting shop or ship–chandlers about these. Always use the latest charts.

Some lighthouses are painted in coloured bands which also help identification. If you intend to spend time on the water in your area, it is as well to learn the colours, flash sequences and sound signals. The time may come when for one reason or another you are caught out there in a fog or in the dark and would have no idea where you were without knowledge of the various signals.

Spritsail barge *Xylonite* passing old-type buoy

Channel markers in harbours and estuaries are set as follows, always assuming that you are arriving, entering the harbour, on a flood tide.

Since 1977 a new Maritime Buoyage System has been installed, replacing some of the eighteen systems at present in use throughout the world. This system is intended to simplify and rationalise the buoyage, and as far as small boat people are concerned it has probably achieved its aims. Some pilots and navigating officers are not so sure that it is an improvement and stress that more than ever it is important to use charts and radar to navigate safely in narrow waters. Of course cruising yachtsmen use charts if not radar, and it must be stressed that because the new buoys have not yet been installed everywhere, and because the responsible authorities have some latitude within the system and are still trying to get the buoys set to the best advantage, it is important to use up-to-date charts and to keep them corrected. The old system may not be replaced round the Scottish coasts and islands and the western Irish coast until 1981. To be safe, familiarise yourself with local buoys and marks if you intend to venture far or to be on the water at night.

The new system has 'Cardinal Marks' which are either pillar or spar buoys and are all in combinations of black and yellow, with two triangular top marks. The setting of the triangles and the colour bands varies according to the position of the buoy in relation to the sand-bank. For instance, should you see a buoy with the top half painted black and the bottom half yellow, bearing two upward pointing triangles, it is a north mark, and the hazard is to its south. So on for the other three points, east, west, and south. Should such buoys mark a large irregular sandbank they will be set on its various corners with the ordinary port- or starboard-hand lateral buoys (see diagram) between them along the sides of the bank. The old middle-ground buoys have gone and the cardinal spars or pillars mark the extremities of banks everywhere.

A black pillar or spar buoy with horizontal red bands is an isolated danger buoy placed on wrecks or submerged rocks. Its top mark is two black balls or discs. These and the cardinal marks flash white lights. Check sequences from a chart.

The lateral marks used to buoy channels are now plain red for port hand and green for starboard hand, with matching lights. Port-hand buoys are either can or spar buoys with single red can top marks. Starboard-hand buoys are conical or spar buoys with single triangle top marks. These buoys are set on the assumption that you are arriving in an estuary or harbour mouth with the flood tide. The marks further offshore are set assuming a general clockwise flood-tidal flow round the land mass and ignoring local flood tide variations. Where this conflicts with the actual approach from seaward convention it will be clearly marked on your chart. So again, a chart is essential.

Plain yellow buoys are now used as special marks, temporary or permanent. They can be spherical, conical, can, pillar or spar buoys but must not be set so that the shape conflicts with conventional marks. In other words a yellow can buoy must not be used on the

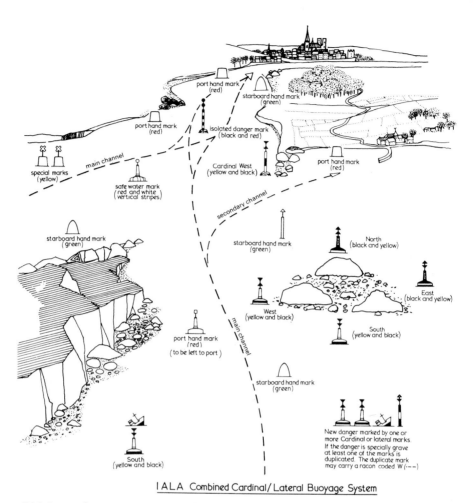

Labels within the figure:

port hand mark (red)

starboard hand mark (green)

isolated danger mark (black and red)

port hand mark (red)

special marks (yellow)

main channel

Cardinal West (yellow and black)

safe water mark (red and white vertical stripes)

starboard hand mark (green)

secondary channel

starboard hand mark (green)

North (black and yellow)

East (black and yellow)

West (yellow and black)

South (yellow and black)

main channel

port hand mark (red) (to be left to port)

starboard hand mark (green)

New danger marked by one or more Cardinal or lateral marks. If the danger is specially grave at least one of the marks is duplicated. The duplicate mark may carry a racon coded W (·−−)

South (yellow and black)

IALA Combined Cardinal/Lateral Buoyage System

IALA new buoyage system: red buoys to port on entering harbours, green to port on leaving

starboard side of a channel, where the buoys are conical, but only on port where the buoys are can shaped. These buoys may all bear a yellow cross top mark and have yellow lights.

A newcomer is the safe water mark. This is a spherical pillar or spar buoy with red and white vertical bands and a single red disc or ball on top. It indicates safe water all around it in places such as anchorage well away from channel markers in open water. It can also be used as a mid-channel mark and sometimes as a landfall buoy. If it has a light it flashes white. Lightships perform the same function as buoys on a bigger scale (see page 50).

One other type of harbour mark which is very important and very useful is the leading mark. Whatever form it takes, either lights on posts, or perhaps black triangles on posts, or even two conspicuous buildings marked on a chart, the principle is that one, when seen from the sea, is higher than the other, and that when they are lined up one above the other, you are moving directly up the channel. These marks can be very useful indeed in shallow estuary water which appears to the eye to be the same depth all over. Fixed leading marks are always marked in on charts and it is quite easy to work out your own for local boating. Church spires lining up with factory chimneys, that kind of thing.

FURTHER READING   Beaver, Patrick. *A History of Lighthouses* (Peter Davies); Jackson, D. *Lighthouses of England and Wales* (David & Charles); Middleton, E. W. *Discovering Lifeboats* (Shire); Riley, Capt R. J. F. *Stanford's Sailing Companion* (Stanford Maritime). (Stanford Maritime publish tidal atlases for harbours, harbour charts, coastal charts for yachtsmen, mainly for the southern half of England. 12-14 Long Acre, London WC2E 9LP.
Imray, Laurie, Norie & Wilson Ltd, Wych House, St Ives, Huntingdon, Cambs. Publishers of charts and guides for yachtsmen.)

USEFUL ADDRESSES   *RNLI,* 21 Ebury Street, London SW1W 0LD; *Yachtsman's Lifeboat Supporters Assen,* 29a Castle Street, Salisbury, Wilts.

4

Small Boats

Coastal Types

All round our coasts, wherever it was possible to get fishing boats to sea, there developed over the years different types of fishing and small working boats, and those who know about such things could specify the home port of such boats just by looking at them. The hulls have shapes developed primarily by use and experience as the best for their own particular purpose. The boat which can be launched in sheltered water and does not have to face big seas is totally different from that which must be launched and recovered through surf, and must either be rowed or sailed through swells or breaking surf to the comparative safety of deeper water.

Boats which are to run into a harbour or on to a sheltered beach where there is no surf, may have square transoms, which take the mountings for outboards very conveniently. Boats with sloping counters or double-ended boats may have the engine mounted just inboard with a trunk down which the propeller and its shaft pass to the water. So the harbour boat, always coming home into sheltered water, is very different from that which must run up a shingle bank, chased by violent and destructive breakers.

A boat which is to be launched and recovered on a shingle bank must have a strong stem and stern to withstand hammering on the beach, should be fairly high sided and may have a rudder which can be lifted out of the way of the beach, and an engine which will lift or, if the engine is inboard, a protected propeller. It should be possible to launch with the rudder shipped as it can be difficult in anything but a calm sea to slip the rudder on to its pintles once the boat is in the water. The stern of the boat should not be a bluff square transom, or as the boat is beached following waves will crash into it and drench everyone.

Much better is a long counter, a lugger stern or a lute stern, which slopes so that the following seas can run up under the boat without splashing, and on launching stern first, the boat rides high over the surf.

High-sided boats give better protection from wind and weather, especially if fitted with a canvas dodger or hood, or built on 'cuddy'. When working nets or pots, high sides can be a nuisance as the gear must be hauled over them, and very stable boats, but with little freeboard, are best. Boats with little freeboard and sloping lines may be very seaworthy, and excellent for launching through surf on sandy beaches, but do not give much shelter from wind and water once out at sea or at anchor, are more likely to ship water and may not be too stable.

Before the days of engines, when boats were rowed or sailed, this too had an effect upon hull designs. The narrow boat was easier to row and control in surf, and the beamier boat more stable under sail. The Deal galleys, narrow and long enough to be rowed by six or more men, also carried sail, and in order to make them stable were ballasted with hundredweights of shingle from the beach. They had flat counters and were launched bows first with sails up. There are only two or three galleys left and it was a sad day some twenty years ago when

Deal fishing boat: note lugger stern, protected propeller, deep bilge keels and neat cuddy – all excellent for work off a shingle bank

three put off for a race in Deal Regatta, were overwhelmed by the conditions and sank to the bottom under their heavy weight of ballast.

All the Deal boats are powered nowadays. Some are used for inshore commercial fishing, netting sprats, longlining for cod, but mostly purely for taking parties of anglers out for a day's sport. Deal is the great centre in the South East for the sport of sea angling, and according to the time of year, enormous cod, tope, and big catches of mackerel are made by the boats. Sea anglers also catch conger eel, pouting, whiting and various types of shad. Perhaps the most sought after in the autumn and early winter are the big cod which still abound on this coast.

Many of the boats are quite old, and were once sailed, but it is interesting that although it is twenty-five or thirty years since fishing boats left Deal beach under sail, such new boats as have been and are being built still retain the basic hull shapes of the old sailing boats, with lugger sterns and very high sides, and with round fat bilges. In fact when I first came to live in Deal, after my Norfolk home and a completely different type of longshore boat (see below), the Deal boats with their high sides looked most ungainly to me. These boats never have to come in on sandy beaches, or through long lines of breakers, and are never launched into heavy seas. If they cannot be got clear by a good shove, stern first, down the tallow-greased planks into

Worthing fishing boat: note the lute stern, lifting rudder and protected propeller

the sea and through the breaking waves just a few yards offshore, then they are just not launched, for if caught even slightly abeam by a big breaking wave they would be hurled back on to the shingle with disastrous results. As it is, the high lugger stern helps the boat to lift as it hits the water. If caught out in a rising sea they make for home, and wait until those on the beach have set up the planks, have a winch running and a wire and hook ready at the water's edge. The boat comes in fast, the rudder is lifted up at the last moment, and the man on the beach hooks the winch cable into the eye low down on the stem, and instantaneously the winch is let in gear and the boat hauled clear. Maybe the first wave will smack into the transom and poop the boat drenching those in it, but by the time the second wave reaches it, it will be yards up the beach and the water will run harmlessly under the sloping stern.

Provided these boats are strongly built with stem, keel, keelson, bilges, ribs and planking to stand this battering on and off shingle beaches, they come to no harm and last for many years.

In the old days the Deal sailing luggers – which were used not only for fishing but as tenders for the hundreds of sailing ships which waited for a fair wind down channel, in the Downs, including the home fleet – could be up to 38ft long and carried quite a lot of sail. They needed to be fast to escape the revenue cutters after them for smuggling, and needed to be seaworthy, even in these comparatively sheltered waters, to make the most they could out of 'hovelling' or supplying the sailing ships.

When I was a child there were dozens of crab boats at Sheringham and Cromer, and only a few of them had engines. Now at Sheringham, there are only a dozen boats all with good engines, yet the hull shape has not changed at all. The crab boats are double ended, that is both ends are sharp, as it were, and although the propeller is protected and the rudder lifts clear, the boats look nothing like the Deal boats described above. Crab boats are very beamy and very stable, as their use is to carry, lay and recover dozens of very heavy crab and lobster pots. Nevertheless their build is comparatively light with many ribs and narrow strakes, and they are not particularly high sided; the bilges run away with a much more graceful profile than that of the tubby Deal boats. These boats are normally launched, bows first, off a shingle bank at high tide (at Sheringham) and often into steep breakers for quite a few yards offshore. They ride over these like seagulls and do not knock back or broach to, their sharp bows cutting the water. On recovery at low water if the seas are rough they run in fast through up

The last of the Deal galleys. This boat has been repaired now and is in the Deal maritime museum. Note transom stern and the extreme length in relation to the beam of this fast rowing and sailing boat

to 200 yards of surf, turn, and then are hauled up the beach on special small rollers like big cotton reels in a heavy wooden frame, the crews hanging on the gunwales to keep the boats upright. However, if a boat is beached in surf and has to wait a bit for recovery, the crew lean on one gunwale to roll the boat so that one bilge is lifted and the sea runs harmlessly beneath, washing the boat inshore.

Further north, up the Yorkshire coast are the cobles. Heavily and strongly built, but long and narrow with a sharp forefoot, these boats launch through surf, stem first, and beach stern first, always presenting a fine sharp bow to the breaking seas. Such boats could not be used off the shingle banks of the south-east coast as they have flat low sterns for ease of beaching on sand, and such sterns would cause the boats to drive straight under if launched down a steep bank.

Down the south coast most of the smaller longshore boats are much the same in type and build as the Deal boats, but with less rounded bilges. One exception is the famous Hastings lugger; once sailed, now all with engines, these boats are 30 or more feet long and weigh around 10 or 12 tons. They are fully equipped motor fishing boats, which on the beach look much too large to be there. However, over the years the hull has been developed exactly for the use to which it is put and the manner of launching and beaching perfected. It is obviously impossible to launch these boats at a run, so they are let down the beach over greased timbers, and held back by a holding anchor dug into the beach. Heavy hawsers or outhauls are anchored well out in the sea and, through the boat's winch, used to haul the boat clear of the beach if necessary. The boat's engine is always going when it reaches the water, and the propeller going astern soon pulls her clear. When she beaches she is hauled up the shingle by a powerful winch, and lies over on one bilge as she slides up the greased timbers. In the old days

Modern fishing boat at Deal being winched out of the sea before the fishing party have disembarked. The high sides of this tubby boat are typical. The planks on which it is pulled up are greased with tallow

recovery was a slower job as it had to be done by a capstan winch, usually worked by a horse being led round in a circle.

And so it goes, right round our coasts. The west-coast and Scottish boats are different again, especially where they have to be launched through heavy surf, and to cope with Atlantic weather conditions. Few of the larger trading boats remain, except for the Thames and east-coast sailing barges, many now fortunately restored and prized for their own special beauty. All are used for pleasure and not for business, but they do still sail and their owners are at great pains to keep their rigs and tackle and fittings authentic in this plastic age.

Acquiring a Small Fishing or Day Sailing Boat

There are three ways to acquire a boat: buy a local secondhand boat, buy a new boat, or have a boat built. Of course there are advantages and disadvantages whichever you do. Study the boats already in use in your area. Designs vary a great deal according to locality and there is always a good reason for these variations. Certainly take into account what your use of the boat will be – rod fishing, longlining, potting, trawling – and take advice from others doing the same thing, and from boatbuilders about suitability. Remember that high-sided boats are much harder to row than are low-sided boats, wide boats harder than narrow boats. If your boat is to be left on moorings then shape of transom is not so important. If the boat is to be trailed away, then weight does become a factor. It is possible to launch and recover singlehanded quite easily from a trailer with a good winch, the boat being wound back on. The limiting factor is how near to the water's edge you can get the boat on its trailer before having to unhitch it from your car and manipulate the trailer by hand. It must be pushed into the water and the boat floated off, and the process reversed on recovery.

Of course the size of your dinghy is important. For runabout use, or use by children, it must not be so big and heavy that it is tiring to row and to pull clear of the water.

For fishing, reckon on about 10ft of length for a one-man boat, and an additional 2ft (which also implies more width or beam) per person. Over 16ft a boat becomes quite a handful to get on and off a trailer and a weight to pull, but it depends on the material of the boat's hull.

Very small 'pram' dinghies are useful tenders in sheltered water, for moving out to a boat on moorings, but must not be overloaded, as there is not much room for the rower anyway. Not to be recommended for fishing.

Sheringham crabbers, double-ended, beamy and graceful. Rudders have been lifted off and the propellers are again protected

Look for good dry locker space for spare clothes, flares, first aid kit, food, water, spare fuel, fishing tackle, ropes, tools, etc. Some modern designs in fibreglass (usually known as GRP, see page 66 for full details of this material) are sadly lacking in this respect. In a boat which has no such storage, everything ends up in a damp tangle. All compartments must have good watertight doors or hatches.

The traditional types of wooden hull are: *clinker* built, in which overlapping planks are attached to the interior ribs, with longitudinal timbers forming a keelson at the bottom and strakes round the top edges or thereabouts; *carvel* built, in which the planks are not overlapped but butted; *laminated* in which the layers of thin plank are laminated together; and *hard chine* in which marine ply is attached to longitudinal members with thwarts and bulkheads forming strengthening and shaping members.

Clinker-built boats are the commonest. Damaged planks can be replaced much more easily than they can in carvel-built hulls (which are not common in fishing boats) and laminated hulls must be patched if damaged, and again are not common in fishing boats. Plywood boats, with the advanced knowledge of the construction methods which has come via the many types of plywood sailing dinghy (now being superseded in far too many cases by GRP), are now much more popular. They are easy for the amateur to make, and quite good for estuary and harbour use, though not perhaps heavy enough to take out into open sea, and not too good for standing up to heavy battering on shingle beaches. The fact that plywood may only be bent into one curve at a time rather limits the lines of boats made from it and the pleasing and seaworthy double curves achieved by traditional building methods and by moulded GRP are not possible.

If you intend to buy a new boat, then a visit to the Annual Boat Show in January, or to one of the regional boat shows which have become such excellent shop windows, provides a chance to look at all types and shapes and sizes of new boat, both in traditional timber construction and in GRP.

On the basis of the traditional designs, there is now a whole new generation of small boats, made of double-skin GRP with built-in buoyancy, timber finished, and with modern synthetic sails as opposed to heavy tanned canvas, modern fittings and standing and running rigging. In fact the use of the latest techniques of boatbuilding and new materials has made it possible for these boats to be produced at competitive prices. To build them out of wood in the traditional ways would be desperately expensive, and the time and expertise required would be far beyond the capacity of the kind of person who now buys these boats.

These GRP boats are lighter than their wooden ancestors and therefore capable of being towed on suitable trailers and launched without difficulty, and are certainly rugged enough to be kept on suitable moorings.

Honnor Marine of Totnes were among the first in the field with their Drascombe lugger, and have developed a whole family of boats. The little Scaffie (see page 79), ideal for estuary sailing, rowing or motoring with the standing lugsail with no boom, easily rolled and reefed right down, makes for safe handling. She has a double-ended hull and her outboard is in fact mounted inboard and works through a well so that it can be hoisted out of the way for sailing and beaching, yet be there for immediate use. An ideal small runabout dinghy. The bigger Dabber carries a mizzen, standing lug, which is loose footed, and a jib on a bowsprit, looks pretty and sails well. It is a nice compromise for sailing, fishing or just pottering. As well as the lugger, there is the Longboat, the Coaster and the Drifter. Both the latter have cabins, the Drifter's including berths, a galley, stowage etc.

Cornish Crabbers of Rock on the Camel estuary make the Cornish Coble (see page 80). This has a pleasing hull shape which is very seaworthy, and is halfdecked with a well aft for rudder and motor. It has two sail plans, both include a standing lug mainsail, used along with the mast set forward for singlehanded work, or with the mast brought back and a fair-sized jib for more lively sailing with a crew. From the same yard come the big Crabbers, a beautiful adaptation of a traditional design carrying the mass of sail which makes such boats interesting sailing indeed for the dedicated traditionalist.

Aquasprint of Sittingbourne are possibly the most adventurous modern makers of traditional boats and by a combination of cold moulding methods can make one-off 'reproduction classics', anything from a Harwich Bawley to an American Slave Trade Schooner, including the absolutely delightful Friesche Tjotter. This is a small yacht of a type originally used for fishing in Holland and now quite common out there for pleasure sailing. This version has a double moulded GRP hull with solid carved English oak fore and after deck, bulkheads, gunwale cappings, lee-boards, etc. Those who know what the marvellous Dutch sailing barges look like, should recognise the Tjotter as a kind of miniature version of these. For sheer looks this boat takes some beating and is fun to sail if not fast. It will float almost in a puddle, drawing only a foot of water, and rests happily on mud or at moorings. Functional certainly, but so much more than that – in fact a dream boat for some, including me.

Two more deserve special mention. First the Orkney boats built at Yapton. These are very basic unadorned GRP boats based on the traditional open Orkney Longliners and smaller Spinners. Very sea-worthy with a high sheer to the bows, good for choppy seas, and the model with a cuddy turns it into an all-weather fishing boat. They go well with small engines, outboard or inboard, and are easy to row. Excellent estuary or inshore boats.

The Devon Dory from Grattons of Starcross is a plywood boat,

Crabber beaching through dangerous surf

Crabber being turned. The winch wire has been hooked on and the crew are 'sitting her down' so that the sea washes her round

unlike the others mentioned, but retains a traditional if rather beamy dory hull shape and can be motored, rowed or sailed. She has buoyancy bags, and is fine for sheltered waters. She would make an excellent boat for youngsters or beginners, or for quiet pottering.

GRP boat hulls can be bought bare and unadorned or in all stages of completion up to the finished boat, which does allow the handyman to save money by doing a lot of his own work, and also to incorporate his own ideas to some extent. GRP needs little maintenance, is easily repaired if damaged, and looks nice when new, although after a bit the surface does lose its sparkle, as it were. The glass fibre boat has quite definitely come to stay, and has good resale value. Whether or not these boats will last for fifty or sixty years as does the well-made wooden boat, yet remains to be seen. To my eye the boats which have plenty of timber 'trim' are the most attractive.

The modern flat-hulled GRP boats with two or three hull ridges under water, are very popular for fishing and are easy to handle on trailers and flat beaches, although not so good in surf. They have the big advantage of being very roomy, and very stable – virtually impossible to capsize. Excellent fishing platforms, in fact.

There are many other small GRP fishing boats on the market; most owe something in design to the traditional fishing boats, but often combine features of several types or are a kind of hybrid general purpose form. Bonwitco of Kingsbridge make an excellent proven range which has a new concept of hull design. Displacement-type hulls sit in the water and are therefore harder to move through it than planing hulls which sit on it (see Power Boating page 74, and Racing Dinghies page 179). This GRP moulded Dromedile hull sets out to combine the safety and sea-going qualities of the displacement hull with the speed and ease of movement (and consequent fuel saving) of the planing hull. The secret seems to be in the slightly concave profile of each hull panel, which looks like imitation clinker building, but is not quite that.

I repeat that the National and Regional Boat Shows are the places to see all the available types and give you a chance to make comparisons and a choice.

Checking a Secondhand Boat

Of course, if you are inexperienced then a marine surveyor can examine the boat of your choice, but he will also charge well for doing the job, and by the time he has examined and perhaps rejected several boats, you would have been better off buying a new one. It is not too difficult to tell if a boat is in reasonable order. The first way is the attitude of the seller. If he does not want you to look too closely at it then there may be something wrong. A boat which has been freshly painted for sale, might also be suspect. A good coat of paint can hide a lot of bad spots. Varnish does *not* hide what is beneath, although it does not last long because it does not have the opacity and light-reflecting qualities of paint.

Check the ribs – none should be cracked. Check all the points such as stem and stern where planking attaches to other timbers. Check along the keelson from the inside and do all this with the sharp point of a knife. Check the trunk where the propeller shaft goes through. If the knife goes into soft wood, then have a good scrape to find out just how bad the timber is. If the owner protests that you are spoiling his paintwork, say 'not today thank you' and look elsewhere.

Check for nail sickness, which is a kind of weeping or bleeding where nails, rivets, screws, etc, enter the timber. It may not be serious, but can, if it has gone on for a long time, cause weak spots which leak continuously.

Wherever water has got under varnish and remained on timber, specially softwood, it causes black stains. These may not be serious, just unsightly, provided the damp is not still getting in. The varnish must be removed and the timber dried out. The stain can be sanded off, or if deep, treated with oxalic acid. The black spots are common but not serious on old oars, masts and spars.

Check all places where iron work is attached to the boat, and make sure that screws, etc, are firm and in firm wood, not just in filler. Check the iron work itself if it has been freshly painted, especially with aluminium paint. Some people are too lazy to chip off rust and clean up properly before repainting especially if they intend to sell the boat to a sucker.

If two different types of metal are touching each other and then immersed in water electrolysis takes place which causes a kind of scabby corrosion. So look out for this if your boat has mixed brass and aluminium alloy fittings, spars, etc.

A boat which has a fixed rudder, that is a rudder which is attached permanently to the boat, or which does not lift up to a horizontal position, may have suffered damage to rudder, rudder fittings and/or transom, if the boat has been carelessly beached. Even if it is the type which drops on to metal fittings, a beaching with the rudder still shipped may cause damage as a great strain is put on the whole apparatus when the weight of the back end of the boat is taken on it. Check thoroughly for any signs of weakness in the transom, rudder and fittings.

If your boat has masts and spars, don't worry about lengthwise cracks or 'shakes' as they are called, wood splits naturally this way as it seasons and is not going to break. Transverse cracks are a different matter, and will inevitably cause breakage sooner or later.

As for such things as ropes and chains, modern synthetic ropes come in all shapes and colours, sizes and breaking strains, and if the boat you buy has these you should be able to check out that they are suitable for the job they are doing, by comparing with new rope at the nearest chandlers. Modern synthetic ropes are very strong, and do not rot in sea water. Older type hemp and sisal ropes have a limited life. Check anchor chains and shackles and links for rust by chipping with a cold chisel; if one tap with a hammer produces a flake of rust and bright metal beneath, don't worry, but if the rust goes deep, then a new anchor chain may be necessary.

Have a good look round inside any lockers with a torch, and as lockers and hatches are opened, get your nose down and sniff; any

Planking replaced on a clinker built hull

wetness or rot will smell unmistakably. Check topsides and angles of decking in case rainwater is getting in from the top.

If the boat has buoyancy tanks – and these are a sensible precaution – be sure that they are watertight. This can only be done by putting the boat in the water and deliberately flooding it. Take out the bungs and get several people to sit in the anchored boat. If the buoyancy tanks are sufficient to hold up the boat and its crew it will not sink. But if the tanks are not watertight the weight of crew and hull will force water into them and the boat will list and/or sink. When the boat is full of water, wait for at least ten minutes to make sure there is no change before replacing the bungs, and bailing out. If this can be done at high tide and the boat left to take ground as the tide goes out, with the bungs still out, she will drain naturally without damage. Never try to check a boat for watertightness by filling it with water when it is high and dry. This puts an intolerable strain on the hull and will probably damage it.

If a boat has been left out of the water for any length of time it may have suffered much damage from drying out and warping, and there may be bad leaks between the planks of a clinker-built boat which has got too dry. The owner may claim that a bit of caulking and a few hours in the water will put all that right and the boat will 'plumb up'. It probably will not!

Small engines, either outboard or inboard, can be very troublesome, except when brand new, especially if they have not been well maintained or kept covered and as salt free as possible. Be sure that secondhand engines work properly and that any electricals, batteries, plug leads, etc, are in proper order. Here the expert mechanic is the only man to check out an engine for you if you yourself have no knowledge.

Most of all this is commonsense and there is little which cannot be mended or cured with ingenuity, expertise and hard work. Much can be done with modern plastic fillers and sensible replacement of bad timbers and some good patching. Provided you have not paid too much for the boat it might be well worth repairing. It is just a case of knowing perfectly well that you are buying a boat which needs repairing.

When buying boats, as with a lot of other things, it is surprising

(Opposite)
Drascombe dabber fitted with jib, gaff mainsail and mizzen. Offset outboard engine mounted inboard. No cuddy *(Honnor Marine)*

what can be found out by casual word over a pint of beer in the local, about why a boat is for sale and what is its history. Boats which may look quite new may be years and years old, and none the worse for that, as they were hand made to last in those days.

Power Boats

The choice of boat depends on what it is to be used for. A family runabout for coastal, estuary or river cruising, need not be fiercely powerful, but should be reliable and stable, especially if it is to be used moored for fishing. In which case a beamy boat with a flat or concave 'cathedral' bottom or a design which is multihulled under water can be best.

Racing power boats are a different matter and not in the scope of this book.

Modern Cornish crabbers *(Cornish Crabbers Ltd)*

A boat for towing water skiers should be capable of good acceleration, and needs a fair amount of power to pull skiers along at the speeds they need (see Waterskiing page 190). It should be stable and not too high sided so that skiers can climb in from the water without great effort. There are plenty of boats available which can be used for cruising, fishing and waterskiing, and the best place to see them and make a choice is at a boat show. Choice may depend somewhat on whether the boat is to be left on mooring, or taken out of the water on a trailer, left near at hand or trailed for a considerable distance. Obviously a big boat and trailer needs more people, a more powerful winch, a more powerful car to handle it, so compromise may be the thing. A V-shaped hull is best for fast work, but any type which is capable of reaching the required speeds can be used for towing skiers.

A power boat is essentially a planing boat. Motor fishing boats with speeds under 15mph chug along with the whole of their bottoms in the water (displacement hulls), but any boat with the appropriate shaped hull which can go faster than that, does at about that speed 'hump', in other words its bows go up as it rides on to its own bow wave and then it settles on the front of that wave with the bows slightly raised and at least half the hull bottom out of the water (planing hull). Friction is thus enormously reduced and the boat can theoretically go even faster. Wind and wave conditions control just how fast you can push a boat without thumping it to pieces. To develop the necessary power a 13ft boat needs an engine of at least 18hp and usually waterskiing boats have a much more powerful engine than that.

SECONDHAND BOATS

Because GRP, glass fibre, is capable of being perfectly and strongly repaired, there is no reason why a secondhand boat which has been properly used and looked after should not be a good buy. But if the boat has been abused it may show signs of crazing in the gel or top coat (not necessarily of any concern but a sign of stress nevertheless) and of star cracks where the hull has hit obstructions or where heavy objects inside the boat have bumped about. However, as described on page 91, crazing in the gel coat and star cracks may be a sign that water has got into the hull, and there may be large areas of lamination which will have to be rebuilt. If you look along the hull against the light you may be able to see where it has been patched. Look carefully at any secondhand boat *out* of the water for anything asymmetrical. The foredeck or transom may be distorted, the coamings may not be exactly the same. These faults could indicate a serious collision at some

Orkney Longliner: the high bow makes for a dry boat in a choppy sea *(A. J. Linton)*

time. Seen from the side, the bow may have dropped a little and the boat be 'hooked'. This can be seen more clearly along the lines of the hard chines. Slight hooking is not serious, but anything really noticeable should warn you right off.

If the gel coat on a fibreglass hull has been painted over, then be careful. This may have been done to cover up crazing and a lot of serious blemishes. Certainly, if it has not been done really recently, it should be a warning. However, a new formula of two-can polyurethane paint has recently been marketed which is rock hard and does render the surface waterproof, and if the boat has been painted with this then it is an advantage, and should put the price up rather than lower it.

Check that the wooden trim of a secondhand boat is all hardwood. Some amateur boatbuilders, who have finished a bare hull, have used softwood which is, however carefully sealed, quite unsuitable for almost all marine purposes, neither strong enough nor water resistant enough. Thwarts, gunwales, etc, of softwood will have to be replaced in short order.

Check all fittings carefully. The steering system and its springs and fastenings should be in good order, and seats, etc, properly secured down, *not* with wood screws. Unless you are an expert, engine checking is best left to a qualified mechanic. Check that dashboard instruments all work properly. As described on page 72, have a look inside any enclosed areas, and see that buoyancy of whatever type is not waterlogged and is properly secured and watertight.

Inflatables

Modern inflatables are robust, easy to launch in almost any conditions in which you might want to launch them, take up little space when deflated, and can provide a lot of handling fun once you have experience. They come in all sizes. They are extremely safe craft, having a low freeboard and tremendous buoyancy. The drawbacks are that they are very wet boats in anything of a sea, and give the passengers a bumpy ride in such conditions. They do not ride comfortably to anchor for protracted spells of fishing, as the hull moves all the time to accommodate itself to the shape of the water passing beneath and round it. Even with protective dodgers they are cold, and storage of quantities of gear is not practicable. An inflatable may be used to tow water skiers, provided the engine is powerful enough, but

Beaufort inflatable family runabout *(Beaufort)*

wear and tear where the wooden sternboard, which takes the engine and the towing hooks, pulls against the fabric, can be a serious problem. The RFD Zodiac is used exclusively for waterskiing. Some inflatables can be sailed.

Special kits are available with which to mend tears in the fabric, but once punctured, however well repaired, the weak spot remains and may well blow again. When buying a secondhand inflatable beware of the patched boat. Never buy it without taking it on the water with a good load up and giving it an exhaustive test, preferably asking that it be left in the water overnight. Slow punctures and perished or weak spots may not be apparent on quick inspection. Of all types of boat the inflatable probably loses its value quickest and has the shortest life.

Inflatables are favoured by skin divers because they are easy to climb back into, are fast, and excellent in choppy seas, and can be used readily from bigger boats, being easier to launch and recover than wooden or GRP dinghies. Getting wet in an inflatable does not discourage people already in wet suits!

Day Sailers

The dividing lines between dinghy sailing, day sailing and boat fishing are by no means definite, and one may use the same boat to do any or all of these things. Nevertheless there are certain boats designed purely for those who wish to spend a day on the water either in an estuary or at sea, in comfort and safety, yet have interesting sailing. A day sailer should provide endless pleasure and sport for those who do not wish to do their sailing from large marinas complete with supermarkets and all mod boating cons; a day sailer uses his boat to transport him on his chosen water so that he can take photographs, fish, swim, watch birds, sail and enjoy the weather, or just contemplate.

The day sailer by definition does not have sleeping berths or much in the way of storage space, but has some kind of simple arrangement for cooking or stowing a portable cooker, some shelter from the elements, and enough stowage for plenty of spare clothes, cameras, etc, fishing gear, and a certain amount of food and drink. It may have a small outboard or inboard engine. It will have a simple but efficient rig, possibly two masted, and be so designed that it can take reasonably heavy weather without danger. It is not, like a racing dinghy, a boat sailed by strength and balance alone and liable to capsize as punishment for a moment's bad judgement. A good day sailer should be a dry boat, not taking water inboard in choppy seas, should be easy

Drascombe Scaffie, a traditional standing lugsail. The mainsheet tackle makes for light handling. Three rows of reef points and the tack of the sail is simply lashed to the bow thwart *(Honnor Marine)*

to handle and 'kind'. Comfortable when riding at anchor, and not impossible to run ashore and relaunch without an army to help, and capable of sitting happily on mud or sand without falling over on her beam ends. Such boats as the family of Drascombe luggers (see page 79) are absolutely perfect for this kind of use. Boat shows are the places to see these boats, and if you do have a chance to buy something secondhand, then all the comments on pages 69 to 74 and 75 to 77 apply.

Cruising Boats

Unfortunately rising prices have made even the smallest motor or sailing cruiser very expensive and this type of yachting, either pleasure cruising or racing, has become an expensive pastime. A cruiser must be kept on moorings and usually this means in a marina large or small where charges may be high. Those who live by the water are not on the whole so involved with cruisers, whose owners live in them while they use them and probably live many miles away from their moorings. Nevertheless readers interested in cruising boats for any purpose can get masses of information on the subject from the books and associations detailed below.

FURTHER READING   Fletcher and Ladd. *Family Sports Boating* (Pelham); Russell, J. *Yachtmaster Offshore* (David & Charles); *The New Glénans Sailing Manual* (David & Charles); Heaton, Peter. *Cruising* (Penguin); Heaton, Peter. *Sailing* (Pelican); Bowyer, P. *Boat Engines* (David & Charles); Proctor, Ian. *Boats for Sailing* (Macdonald); Clarkson, Henry. *The Yachtsman's A–Z* (David & Charles); Geen, A. F. *A Handbook of Small Boat Cruising* (David & Charles).

BOAT BUILDERS   *Bonwitco,* 38 Ebrington Street, Kingsbridge, Devon TQ7 1DE (Dromedile boats); *Orkney Boats Ltd,* Ford Lane, Industrial Estate, Yapton, Arundel, Sussex; *Cornish Crabbers Ltd,* Rock, Wadebridge, Cornwall; *Honnor Marine (Totnes) Ltd,* Seymour Wharf,

(Opposite)
Cornish Coble: the standing lug has one set of reef points and the mainsheet is on a horse (bar) so that it can travel across the boat when it changes tacks; the bowsprit carries a useful foresail *(Cornish Crabbers Ltd)*

Rye fishing boat on the mud at low water. Four mooring lines prevent her from hitting the harbour wall at high water

Totnes, Devon TQ9 5AJ (Drascombe boats); *Beaufort Air Sea Equipment Ltd,* Beaufort Road, Birkenhead (Inflatables); *Hutchinson, South Western Factors Ltd,* PO Box 4, 43 Pottery Road, Poole, Dorset (Inflatables); *Avon Inflatables Ltd,* Hendy, Pontardulais, Dyfed SA4 1AF. *Aqua Sprint Ltd,* Lower Road, Teynham, Nr Sittingbourne, Kent (Tjotter and others); *Dell Quay Ltd,* Wadham Stringer, Clovelly Road, Southbourne, Nr Emsworth, Hants PO10 8PE (Fishing boats); *P. N. Gratton,* Starcross, Devon.

USEFUL ADDRESS *Yacht Brokers Designers and Surveyors Asscn,* Orchard Hill, The Avenue, Hazlemere, Surrey.

5

Equipment, Trailers, Maintenance and Moorings

Equipping a Dinghy

However reliable your motor, there should always be at least two, and preferably three oars in the boat, with rowlocks which fit them and their plates in the gunwale. Be sure that the oars are neither so short that they barely reach the water unless the rower's arms are stretched out sideways, nor so long that they cannot both be conveniently used at the same time by one rower. Ideally the oars should allow the rower to hold his hands directly out in front of him when the oar blades are just in the water.

Anchor and anchor cable are vital and a good strong 'samson' post or securing point well forward in the boat is important. There are various types of anchor; take local advice on which holds best in local bottom ground. A 'fisherman' allowing 1lb weight of anchor per 1ft length of boat, is as good a general purpose anchor as any. Carry at least 20 fathoms (120ft) of 1½ or 2in rope. The rule of thumb is at least three times the maximum depth of the water you are likely to anchor in, to allow the rope to run at the correct angle from boat to anchor. Thus if the water is at most 30ft deep, then you need 90ft of anchor rope. Man-made rope, although it need not be so big as hemp, is a little more slippery to handle when wet, but takes up less room in the boat and lasts longer. It is sensible to put 1 fathom of medium chain between rope and anchor. The weight of this helps the anchor to lie down and grip the bottom, and the chain will suffer less from wear from a rough bottom. Make sure that the inboard end of the anchor rope is properly attached to the samson post or securing point. It is a little annoying to let out all the rope and then see the end disappearing after the anchor. See that it is properly stowed or coiled without kinks.

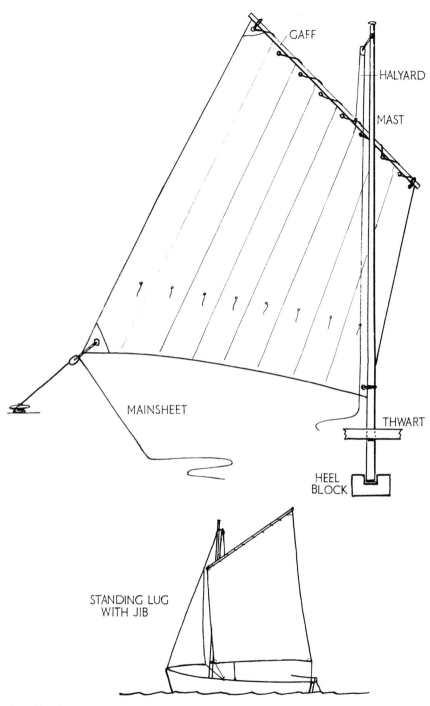

GAFF

HALYARD

MAST

MAINSHEET

THWART

HEEL
BLOCK

STANDING LUG
WITH JIB

Standing lug

An open fair-lead on the bow through which the rope can be passed allows the boat to be properly anchored by the bows. The anchor should be stowed where it can cause damage neither to crew nor to boat, by being trodden on or knocked down.

So many people are prepared to rely solely on an engine, and then find that if it fails they can get nowhere rowing against tide or current. A small sail, permanently set up on gaff and mast, rolled round them both and stowed under a thwart could mean that one day you could sail to safety rather than have to wait for rescue on the end of an anchor. In any case it is pleasant to sail sometimes and save fuel, and sailing is not in the least difficult to learn.

To set up a standing lugsail all that is needed are: a stout mast, two thirds the length of the boat, which drops through a hole in the forward thwart so that the heel or base rests in a housing on the keelson; a cleat low down on the mast above the thwart to take the halliard, and an eye higher up to which to lash the tack of the sail; a short gaff or yard about half the length of the mast with an eye firmly attached a quarter of its length from the forward end; and a sail with a cringle in each corner and eyelets along the head to take the line which lashes the sail to the gaff. The sail needs to be four sided and cut to fit the mast and gaff when set up, with reef points, but need not be a masterpiece of the sailmaker's art. Provided it has been properly sewn with a bolt rope in the head, and with strengthened corners to take cringles for lashings, sheet, etc, it will work. A block attached to the top of the mast, or a single sheave fitted in it, carries a halliard to haul up the gaff and sail. The mainsheet is attached to the transom then passed through a block attached to the cringle at the bottom rear corner or clew of the sail. It is a simple matter to 'step' this mast and sail by dropping the mast through the hole in the forward thwart. Pull the gaff up with the halliard till the sail is taut, then attach the mainsheet to the boat. The boat will sail before the wind or on a reach and there should be no difficulty in finding someone to instruct you in the basics of helmsmanship. This is an extremely simple set-up and can be much improved upon. A small jib as shown in the diagram makes the boat able to sail closer to the wind and to tack much better, and a single whip block and tackle mainsheet is lighter to handle.

There should always be flares in a watertight packet in a dry place in the boat. Yacht-chandlers sell these and will advise on type. If you are likely to be anywhere where shipping of any kind is moving about – ferries, coasters, or big fishing trawlers, anything which might have radar – attach a metal tetrahedron or at worst hoist a metal bucket to the top of the mast if you get caught in a fog. Radar *might* pick it up and a collision be avoided, although small boats low in the water are hard to distinguish on a radar screen from wave tops, buoys, etc.

If you are likely to be on the water in foggy weather, or in a place where fog and sea mist is common, then an aerosol klaxon hooter of the type used by sailing clubs to start races, comes in useful to warn others of your presence, or with which to signal for help.

Always carry a good general first aid kit, extra jumpers, and a couple of modern climbers' survival blankets. It goes without saying that everyone should wear a lifejacket, or at least have one stowed in the boat. A packet of seasickness pills might turn out to be useful. Plastic boxes with snap-on lids make excellent containers.

A small fire extinguisher is essential in a boat with an engine or stove of any kind.

A plastic jerrican or bottle of clean drinking water, renewed frequently as water gets very stale, should always be carried for emergencies. You are not likely to die of starvation in coastal water or estuaries but can get extremely thirsty very quickly indeed. In spite of general beliefs to the contrary, drinks of spirits do not help at all when you are very cold. Hot drinks are the answer. So always keep a little Calor gas cooker, a single burner on a small cylinder, in the boat, and a small kettle, and some tinned or dried milk and cocoa, tea, coffee or Ovaltine, or a bottle of Bovril.

If the boat has an engine always carry a set of *new* sparking plugs, and if it has a starting cord, carry a *new* spare. Carry shear pins or springs for the propeller, and a basic tool kit with which all nuts, screws, etc, on the engine could be shifted if necessary; a good knife, a shackle spanner and some pieces of lashing; some screws of sizes used in the boat; and a spare can of fuel, in an approved can, carefully and properly closed and stowed.

A length of rope which can be used as a painter or tow rope should also be carried. Take advice on type and breaking strain of this from a yacht-chandler, having reference to the size and weight of your boat; 25ft should be long enough.

If your boat is to come alongside piers or jetties or other boats, then she will need fenders; these can range from highly coloured plastic sausages specially made for the job, to bits of old motor tyre hung on ropes. The latter, while effective enough, do tend to make dirty black marks on smart paintwork, usually that of other, prouder owners!

For night fishing of course proper lights should be carried, and a good torch with a waterproof cover can be extremely useful. The type of lamp or lantern to be used is immaterial, but it must be reliable, easy to light, not likely to be put out by wind and weather, and you must carry spare fuel for it. Paraffin is the cheapest and easiest in lanterns and lights with simple wicks for navigation and riding lights. For very bright lights, pressure lanterns are excellent. Calor gas lanterns working from a self-contained cylinder are fine but do be sure the cylinder contains enough gas or that you have a spare.

Trailers

Power boat trailers should be big and strong enough to carry something in the region of a quarter of a ton, including boat, engine, spare gear, etc, so any old trailer will not do if it is to be taken on the road. Brakes, lights, hitch and springing must be in proper order, and axles and bearings in good condition. Over a certain weight, independent braking systems must be installed. A trailer that is used for launching has sand and salt water getting into its axle bearings so must be properly greased and maintained; tyres must be in good condition and are kept at about 50psi, much higher than ordinary car tyres. The winch is an essential part of the trailer for launching and recovery so should be efficient and in good order. Chocking must fit the bottom of your boat exactly and must be well padded, and a trailer with docking arms at the back can be extremely helpful if you intend to launch and recover anywhere where there are even quite small waves or a lateral current. They prevent the boat from swinging sideways off the trailer before it has (a) been run back into the sea clear of the trailer, or (b) been winched right up so that it is in the carrying position on the trailer. Boat shows are the places to inspect different types of trailer, and manufacturers of power boats will often recommend a suitable make or type.

A good trailer is an expensive item, but a boat loaded so that it is properly balanced reduces wear and tear on the towing vehicle considerably. For the same reason braking systems should be in very good order. Do not try to tow a big boat with a small car; the car just will not take it for very long.

Trailers for dinghies need not be so heavy and strong, and may not be big enough to be required by law to have their own braking systems. However, a number plate on a board with duplicate rear lighting exactly as is required by law on the rear of your car, is essential, and must be properly secured and connected up. A piece of board with the number roughly chalked on it just will not do.

Various types of launching trolleys are available for small boats, with axles that are not affected by water provided they are kept greased, but are not usually suitable for road trailing.

Laying up and Maintenance

WOODEN BOATS

At the end of the season, do not just take your boat out of the water and leave it on a trailer, or in a shed, either with or without cover. Make sure that it is clean, drained and dry. Open up all hatches, remove all drain plugs, mop out water and sand which cannot drain out, and leave the boat either upside down or chocked up, well supported on chocks, so that any remaining water or rainwater arriving on the hull can drain straightaway, and not puddle in the bottom. Light boats can be left standing on their transoms. Water will penetrate any varnish if left lying on it long enough, and should it get frozen does all kinds of damage. Where the undersides of enclosed compartments were not

Sailing barge beyond repair moored next to – one that is being rebuilt to sail again

properly varnished when the boat was built (and this is a common fault) moisture which has soaked into the wood appears on the underside of the varnished topsides as a dark patch, and if frost gets into this it lifts the varnish anyway. Such dark patches can only be cured by stripping off the varnish and allowing the wood to dry right out before revarnishing.

Check your boat for any signs of trouble, nail sickness (see page 70), splits, rust on metal fittings, hull damage of any kind, and make a note to repair it before next season. Remove all ropes, check for wear and wash them thoroughly in fresh water, then hang them to dry before coiling them neatly and stowing them away. Clean and grease all brass fittings. Remove and coil up shrouds and leave them soaking in oil with a little petrol or paraffin added to make it run easier, so that the insides of the laid strands get thoroughly coated with the rust-preventing oil. Be careful not to leave this inflammable concoction where it might take fire.

Remove all other fittings and clean and stow them in a dry place. Label standing and running rigging and fittings as you remove them if you are at all likely to be confused next spring when refitting. Any shackles, split rings, bottle screws, etc, which have to be undone should immediately be done up again, attached to the removed fitting so that they have not disappeared by next year. Check all safety equipment; buoyancy bags for leaks, etc, before deflating and storing them with just a little air inside. Check flares to see that they are still dry and usable. Check the first aid kit and store it dry for next year. Remove water and fuel cans and store empty and clean. Service the engine and store it dry and clean. Check the oars and spars, and store them flat, or properly supported along their lengths so that they cannot sag and distort. Metal and wooden masts particularly must be carefully supported. If hung under a roof then have ties up to the roof at 3ft intervals all along the length of the mast.

Generally speaking, however small or large the boat, whatever its type, clean it and dry it, and remove all removable things, and store everything properly till needed again. Make a note of work to be done.

For instruction on stripping down old paint and varnish and repainting or varnishing wooden hulls, look in specialist books, and in the helpful booklets issued by paint manufacturers. For repairs to hull, sails and engines there are specialist books and continual articles in yachting and boating magazines of which there are many such as *Motor Boat and Yachting, Yachting World, Yachting Monthly* and *Practical Boat Owner.*

Many boats are made of glass fibre nowadays and it is not particularly difficult to repair, so that most people do their own work. Unlike wood, damage to the hull does not mean that a whole area of planking or sheathing and possibly its supporting internal timbers must be removed and replaced – craftsman's work is best done in a boatyard. All kinds of holes and dents in GRP can be repaired simply by cutting out the damaged area and refilling it with glass fibre which will be just as strong as the original hull, and if done properly, quite invisible. Scratches can be filled with gel coat, or if slight, painted over.

GRP hulls are made by layering mats of chopped glass fibre with polyester resin, hardened by a catalyst, on to a specially made and perfectly prepared mould, usually a hull made of cheap wood. Experience with laminating GRP hulls, and extended use of them, is however showing up some problems which manufacturers may be reluctant to talk about. The quality of a laminated hull depends upon the skill with which the resin was applied. All air bubbles must have been pressed or rolled out and the outer finish of gel coat must be perfect and properly cured. It is possible to find hulls which are perfect on one side, on the other side of which the laminations are breaking up, one man having been more skilled at applying resin than his mate working on the other side of the boat. Water getting into the laminations and moving by capillary action does them no good and the gel coat must keep water out. However, the disturbing discovery has been made that the gel coat is not quite as waterproof as it might be and that by osmosis (the tendency of a fluid to pass through a semi-permeable membrane into a solution where its concentration is lower), water will, after some years, have passed through into the laminations. It seems possible that not all crazes and stars on the surface of a hull may be due to bumps and stresses alone, but to minute quantities of water behind the gel coat. The answer to this is a new and extremely effective, totally waterproof two-can polyurethane paint for fibreglass which can be applied to brand new or repaired hulls. This 'Perfection 709' has been developed by International Paints.

For repairs, all yacht suppliers and chandlers sell the necessary materials; resin catalyst, glass fibre mat, woven rovings, abrasive cleaners, rubbing compounds, etc. International Paints have produced and will supply free *The Manual of Glassfibre Maintenance* which tells you absolutely everything you need to know about the care, repair and painting of glassfibre boats. This is such a good booklet that no yacht owner should be without and it can be obtained from International

Paint agents. The longevity of fibreglass boats is still to be proved. Some say it will not last as long as wood.

Moorings

If you have acquired a large and valuable boat which must be kept available for immediate use, then it will have to be on a mooring or in a marina, and in these days when demand exceeds supply, either can be very expensive. Such moorings are obtained by approaching the local harbour master or the office of a marina, and do not concern us here.

Moorings for a small boat which is inconvenient for you to pull out of the water every time it is used are a different matter, and there are still plenty of harbours and estuaries where it is possible to obtain or lay moorings for use at least during the summer months. Always ask the harbour master's permission and advice, if there is a harbour master. On creeks and estuaries where none exists, local enquiry should lead you to whoever it is whose permission you must seek, and someone will usually tell you in no uncertain terms where you may *not* lay a mooring. In any case, local knowledge can point out the problems: strong tides and currents, underwater obstructions, interference with the comings and goings of other water users, lack of shelter in certain winds. A mooring should always be where it is protected from prevailing winds and also from direct wave action. Heavy seas coming right in will soon cause trouble. Your mooring should not be too near other boats, where your own boat might damage them as it swings to wind and tide. In a tidal estuary where the water goes far out, it is rather pointless to moor your boat where it will be left high and dry half the time. Favoured moorings in such places are where there is enough water to float the boat at all states of the tide, yet out of the strongest run of current and sea and prevailing wind. Moorings laid in a channel, but too near shallow water may result in the boat swinging across the shallow water and being stranded there as the tide goes out.

The size of your mooring depends on the maximum depth of water, on how exposed it is and on the type of bottom. A mooring usually consists of two heavy anchors of a type which will hold in the local bottom, each with a heavy chain joined to a third chain or riding scope, twice the depth of maximum high water. This riding scope is shackled to a mooring line which is attached to a small buoy with a ring or loop on top of it.

This buoy is picked up and the line pulled inboard through a fairlead

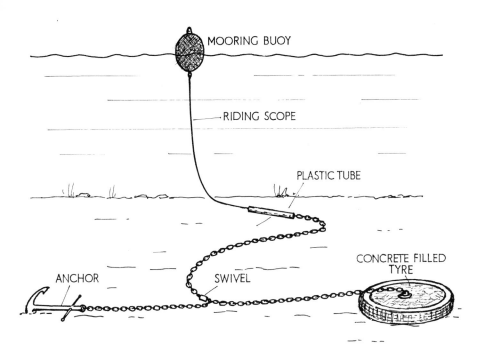

MOORING BUOY

RIDING SCOPE

PLASTIC TUBE

CONCRETE FILLED TYRE

ANCHOR

SWIVEL

Mooring

and made fast inside the boat, usually round a samson post. Slip some plastic hose over the top of the mooring chain where it rubs against your boat so that it does no damage to paintwork.

Anchors being very expensive, large concrete blocks are frequently used to make moorings for small boats. A big motor tyre laid flat and then it and its centre filled with concrete, makes a good heavy mooring. Set a big ring bolt in the middle of the concrete to take the riding scope. A couple of these set a few yards apart make good moorings for small fishing boats, dinghies or power boats, and will take quite a bit of dragging. These blocks, being rubber tyred, are easy to handle on shore and in your boat before laying, whereas solid unprotected concrete is difficult to move about and can so easily damage both boats and crews. If a heavier mooring is needed, then just add extra tyres of concrete, or use lorry tyres.

Of course one large block with a chain or rope on it, buoyed at the surface will do to moor a small boat during calm weather, but cannot be relied on to hold when the wind and sea get up. Even very strong modern synthetic ropes will chafe and pull under continual strain, and it is much better to use chain as described above.

FURTHER READING   Lewis, John. *The Repair of Wooden Boats* (David & Charles); Warren, N. *Outboard Motors Handbook* (Stanford Maritime); Newnes Question and Answer series: *GRP Boat Construction, Wooden Boat Construction,* and *Steel Boat Construction*; Lewis, J. *Small Craft Construction* (Granada); Fry, E. *The Shell Book of Knots and Ropework* (David & Charles); *The Manual of Glassfibre Maintenance* (International Paints).

USEFUL ADDRESS   *International Paints Ltd,* 24/30 Canute Road, Southampton SO9 3AS.

6

Fishing

There are several dozen different species of fish to be caught around our coasts and in our estuaries, from great gleaming salmon and sea trout, sinister conger and beautiful mackerel, to fat little dabs, and there are just as many types of tackle and ways to fish. There are probably hundreds of books about fishing and sea angling which give in great detail types of tackle, habits of fish and fishing methods. All I can do here is to give in the widest sense, information about fish and tackle, and to detail some of the methods of catching fish 'longshore' which are not purely 'sport fishing'.

Including freshwater fishing, someone has calculated, upon what basis I know not, that more people go fishing each weekend than watch football. One cannot think of two more different pastimes, and the enormous appeal of fishing is not really surprising. Few people fish because otherwise they would not eat, although most fish, fresh and well cooked, is delicious. Fish deep-freeze well, so nowadays less of the catch is wasted. Unlike some freshwater anglers, sea and estuary fishermen do not measure their catch, weigh them and put them back, and it seems a shame that the least edible fish are still brought ashore to die and feed the gulls.

Perhaps the greatest appeal of fishing is that it is totally unpredictable; nothing is cut and dried. There is no absolutely right or wrong way to catch anything, no rules. Every individual learns by experience and observation and application how to fish, how to catch the specific type of fish he seeks, yet the unpredictable can and frequently does happen. There are no close seasons at sea, although fish come and go as their spawning seasons and chosen places dictate, and again there are no really hard and fast rules about their movements.

Although sitting on a beach or on a pier with a pub at the end of it, in summer sunshine, and occasionally getting up to reel in and cast again,

The catch taken on one longline

can be restful in the extreme, rocking about in a small boat at anchor, in freezing rain or cold, or sitting it out all a winter's night when the rain is like icy needles and that same pub is shut, is just piscatorial masochism.

How much the hunting, killing instinct motivates fishermen, I do not know. Fishing can certainly be indulged in without much in the way of guilt feelings, for fish cannot scream. The idea that because they are cold blooded they cannot feel pain is utter nonsense, as anything with a nervous system can feel pain. To leave fish to suffocate after they have been caught is reprehensible but is unfortunately more often than not what happens. Fishing is just as much a blood sport as shooting, coursing, or other field sports that are widely condemned. This is not necessarily to condemn fishing which has always been a part of man's life and brings enormous pleasure to millions of people all over the world. No fisherman likes to go home empty handed, but nevertheless a whole day which results in nothing more than a tiddler can bring just as much pleasure as a day when one only has to drop a hook in the water for a fish to grab it. The French adore fishing and any little piece of water big enough to drop a hook in has its quota of anglers. I was leaning over the estuary wall at low tide at St Valery sur Somme, nothing but a shallow creek about 100 yards wide in miles and miles of mudflat. There were, for I counted, at least 150 men and women casting across this creek and reeling in, fishing along the bottom for dab or flounder I suppose. During half an hour not one fish was caught for all that effort. I remarked in my fearful French to a Frenchman also leaning on the wall, 'Plenty of fishermen, no fish', and he rocked with laughter and said, 'But Madame it is the same all over France'. Definitely it is the thought of catching fish, not necessarily the fact, that draws all those hopefuls out to the water. The thought of something for nothing, the thought of that record fish which lurks out there beneath the murky water, even the fact that you cannot see what is happening down there makes it exciting.

Tackle

Much of the tackle on display in the tackle shop window is there to catch the angler rather than the fish. Splendid new rods and reels and associated gadgets *may* help catch bigger and better fish, but they certainly *don't* guarantee it. There is no such thing as a general purpose rod, specialist gear being needed for such things as conger eels. Long rods are a nuisance in a boat, but essential for beach fishing and pier fishing where extra leverage is needed to make long casts.

The old–type reels with central axles and braking systems are still in use by thousands of anglers, but modern fixed-spool reels to which the line is recovered by a bail arm, and which have a slipping clutch, are nowadays considered to be the most efficient type of reel where any long–distance casting is involved.

Modern rods are made of solid or tubular glass fibre, are very strong indeed, and extremely flexible. The changes in rods and tackle over the years have been in materials rather than in type, and modern synthetics are very strong. A given rod reacts perfectly when used with line of specific breaking strain and weight of terminal tackle, and this can be based on the test curve of the rod. This is the pull, measured on a spring balance, which takes the tip of the rod over at right angles to the butt. The weight of pull is then multiplied by five to give the breaking strain. A rod with a test curve of 2lb would have a breaking strain of

10lb. Allow a tolerance of 25 per cent either way. Such a rod would be useless for big fish.

Therefore you must know within reason what you intend to fish for, and, taking the advice of your tackle shop or someone who really knows what he is talking about, buy accordingly.

Different terminal tackles, floats, leads and hooks are necessary for different fishing methods and different fish, but there is no need to buy everything all at once. Just get what you need and gradually build up a stock of good tackle for all eventualities.

Bait Digging

When the tide has gone out across the flats the fisherman has his chance to dig bait. The most common worm for bait is *arenicola marina,* locally known as the lugworm or lobworm. These are brownish red with a tail rather like an earthworm, a body with thirteen pairs of red gills and a little mouth at the head end. Yellowtails are another type of

Conger eel: this one attacked the fisherman just after the photograph was taken *(Basil M. Kidd)*

A record bass *(Basil M. Kidd)*

lugworm which grow larger and have yellowish tail sections, and are very much liked by fish, so are prized as bait.

Lugworms thrive in hard muddy sand, particularly near the mouths of estuaries. They live in U-shaped burrows and on the surface can be detected by the coiled strings – like heaps of worm casts – which are ingested sand and mud from which they have extracted what nutrition they need, before, at precise 40-minute intervals, excreting it up to the surface. The other end of the burrow is marked by a shallow depression where the sand is being sucked down.

These burrows go down about 18in in the sand, and the worm is usually fairly near the surface where the sand contains edible particles. But as soon as it feels the pressure of footfalls or of digging, it retreats to the bottom of the burrow. When the tide begins to come in across the flats, the worm responds to the pressure of the advancing water by moving up towards the surface (although it never leaves its burrow). For this reason the last half hour before the tide reaches your diggings is often the most fruitful, as the worms are near the surface and therefore easier to dig.

Yellowtails live nearer to the low water mark, and their burrows are deeper, down to 2ft. Therefore they are easier to find at low water spring tides, for the half hour before and after dead low water. They also like slightly less muddy sand than common lugworms, so can be found further away from muddy river mouths.

The lugworm digger occasionally finds ragworms as he digs, but on the whole they prefer sandier beaches around estuaries.

The lugworm releases its spawn into the sea on the flood tide and this is then carried higher up the beach. The 'brood' hatches and buries itself in the hard sand high up the beach and proceeds to grow in shallow burrows. Where there is plenty of brood there will be thousands of small worm casts. Unfortunately, eager fishermen, not understanding the life-cycle of the creature, dig up these little worms, not really much good for bait, and so seriously deplete the renewal stock of lugworms, which when they grow to be about $2\frac{1}{2}$ to 3in long, emerge from their burrows and move down into the muddier sand nearer the sea, make new burrows and stay there for the rest of their lives, unless unfortunate enough to be dug up.

Over digging of mature worms, combined with any digging at all of brood, eventually causes the lugworm population to decline to the point where it is not able to keep up with the depredations of diggers. Fortunately this usually forces all but a few diggers, and certainly all commercial diggers, to go elsewhere, and the stocks gradually regenerate. It takes from five to nine years for the stocks to get back to natural levels according to how much digging still goes on.

Bait digging is backaching, wet, heavy, hand-shattering work. An ordinary garden fork with short tines will do but special lugging forks with long handles can be bought. It takes a strong man to wield one of these for very long; the professional diggers usually have the tines shortened a little and honed to a flat point. The bigger the fork the more sand it picks up at a 'bite', so the heavier the work.

Wear old gloves or mittens in the winter to protect the hands from the ravages of sand, sea water and worm juice. Blisters will happen, it is just a matter of getting your hands hardened. Wear wellington boots, an old anorak and a woolly hood to protect you from the weather.

Find a spot with plenty of big worm casts as near to the sea as possible, and as dry as possible, and start digging. Cut a trench about two spits wide and go down about two forks deep and you should immediately find one or two worms. Look in the cut sides and back of the trench for the tell-tale rust-coloured burrow holes and if you see one, immediately take out a spit to include it, digging back a bit from the hole, or you may cut the worm in half. As you drop the sand beside the trench it will break open, and you should see the worms. Pick them

(Opposite) A fine plaice *(Basil M. Kidd)*

100

up instantly and drop them in a bucket. Work backwards until the worms get few and far between. They have sensed you and retreated to the bottom of their burrows. Move 10 or 15 yards away and start again.

Only dig the worms you need. Those not used the same day *can* be kept in a refrigerator for a couple of days, but they do stink.

When you do straighten your aching back there will be gulls and waders about at a discreet distance, waiting for your departure so that they can immediately pick over the diggings for their share of the loot. On a cold winter's morning with the sun just coming up and snow squalls obliterating the landscape every ten minutes or so, the oyster catchers fly low in whistling parties along the sands, and the waders almost ignore your presence as they feed. The bird watcher finds that bait digging is a good way to get out among the birds on sand and mudflat, and as long as he keeps working they will move nearer and nearer in their incessant search for food.

Longlining

To catch fish without actually being there, and to catch fish in quantity, either to sell, or perhaps to fill a few deep-freezers, longlining is an excellent method. Setting longlines from a boat in deep water, over ground which is not exposed at low tide, can produce good catches of fish such as cod in their season. Commercial fishermen use lines from 30 to 60 fathoms long, but 15 or 20 fathoms of 6 or 9 thread sisal should be plenty when fishing for the pot. The longline should be strong, strong enough to haul the dinghy over as it is recovered. A weight of about 8lb is attached at each end. At 1-yard intervals or slightly longer, long snoods or pieces of line each with a swivel and hook are attached to the main line by means of a clove hitch or a special detachable clip. The idea of the detached snood clip is that if when the line is being hauled a fish is brought up deep hooked, in order to save time and to keep up the rhythm of the hauling, it can be detached snood and all from the line and the hook removed later. These are baited with squid, sand eel, or any other appropriate bait for the fish you are after. As the hooks are baited, the line is carefully coiled in a tin bath or tub so that it can be paid out without tangling when the line is set, the tub being turned regularly while shooting the line. Or use Leakey Longline which is a system of rack and bait troughs. It is effective and saves a lot of tangling if used properly, and stores the longline neatly before and after use. The weighted end of the line is

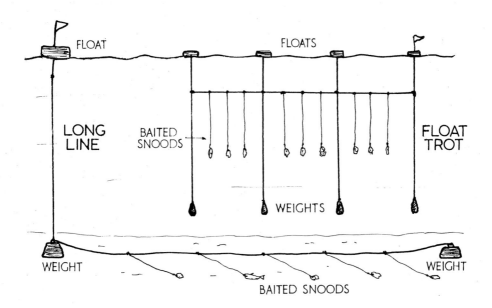

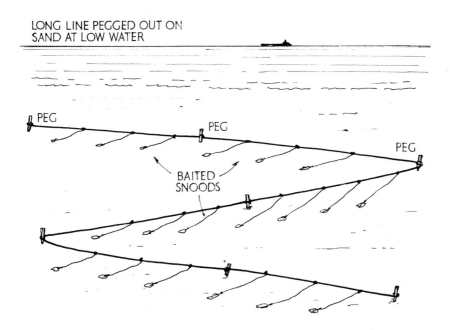

Longlining: *(above)* offshore; *(below)* at low water

thrown over at right angles and the boat allowed to drift downtide or rowed or motored quietly along as the line is paid out. Some fishermen put a sheet of metal over the side to allow the line to run without the hooks catching on the boat. When the other weighted end is reached, attach a strong line with a buoy or marker on the end of it; this should be long enough to stream out at high tide without being pulled under, about three times the depth of the water being fished.

Check the line after a while, hauling it against the tide and removing the fish as the line comes in. If you intend to reset it immediately, then rebait and coil the line as you bring it into the boat.

When fishing for fish nearer the surface, a float trot can be used. This is a series of vertical lines each with a cork float at the top and a weight at the bottom, joined at 1-fathom intervals by a horizontal line just under the surface from which hang the snoods and their hooks.

Longlines may be used very effectively to fish the ground between low and high water, over a gently shelving bottom of sand or mud. The line is put out at low tide in shallow furrows and firmly pegged down at regular intervals, to prevent the line rolling as the tide comes in and thus tangling the snoods and fouling the hooks. It should be zigzagged inshore to cover a wide area of the sand. The snoods with their baited hooks are left lying on the surface. As the sea comes in and covers the lines, the snoods will stream shorewards without tangling. Longlining on the beach needs some care as seagulls may try to take the bait, and when the tide recedes again you must be there to collect your catch or the seagulls will have it as soon as it appears in the shallow water.

Estuary Fishing

Fish are unpredictable, so occasional specimens of almost any species may be caught in estuaries. On the whole only *salmon* and *sea trout* on their way into spawning rivers, and those fish which actually like brackish water and muddy bottoms, come regularly into estuaries or move up river. The *flounder* particularly may find his way well upstream, and trolling from a boat or drifting a baited hook down current is a favourite way of fishing for these flatfish. Flounder lie in gullies and wait for food to drift past their noses, except that they are extremely inquisitive and will go out to investigate disturbances on the sea bed, such as that caused by the trace as it drags across the bottom. The Frenchmen at St Valery (page 97) were fishing for flounder by casting a weight across the river and then slowly reeling

Thornback ray *(Basil M. Kidd)*

in. The disturbance of the weight and a trace with several baited hooks might cause a flounder to investigate and take a bait. They abound from March to November.

Bass can be caught in estuaries from the Wash southwards round to Wales. They like warm water, sand and muddy estuaries and fast-running tideways. Best months are May, June, September and October, although round the south-west coast they may be caught all year round. They can be fished for in many ways and will take many types of bait, which makes them a fish favoured by anglers.

Cod like estuaries over sand but will not go up into brackish water, and abound in autumn and winter. They go off to spawn in the New Year.

Conger Eel is a fish which remains fairly static in his home during the daytime, from whence he ambushes passing fish. Conger often find what to them are attractive homes in underwater crevices, old wrecks, corners under jetties, piers, and even sewerage pipes, so can be found in harbours and estuaries. Summer and autumn are the best time for conger fishing. Congers emanate evil, having fearsome teeth, which if set into the hand of an unwary angler, do not readily let go. They can grow to an enormous size, and there are those fishermen who are eternally dedicated to catching the biggest recorded conger. The rod record at the moment is 109lb, 129in in length. Bigger fish are netted bearing the scars of having been hooked, and every conger fisherman has a tale of the huge beast that broke his tackle. A short rod with a line of at least 80lb breaking strain is essential for conger fishing. Very often caught when fishing for other things, their strength soon breaks lighter tackle, and a conger which has managed to get back into its lair is almost immovable however strong the tackle.

I remember the reaction of my three-year-old daughter to the sight of an unexpected small conger thrashing its way up the shingle beach on the end of a line. She rushed to me as fast as her small legs could run, saying in terror but hopefully, 'Mummy, Mummy, it's only a worm, isn't it?'

Dabs, small and succulent flatfish, frequent sandy ground and come inshore except in deep winter, and are at their best from September to November. They can be caught in sandy estuaries.

Garfish, long and narrow and rather ugly, nevertheless provide good sport and can sometimes be caught in brackish estuary water, in warm spring weather when they move inshore to spawn.

The thick-lipped *grey mullet* which often swims near the surface can actually be seen moving up into salt-water estuaries, creeks and harbours, from March to November. As the fish swim they turn in the sunlight, and one catches a bronze flash. They swim so near the surface that they make characteristic V-shaped ripples. They like sheltered lagoons and sheltered bays and will go right up to where the fresh water meets the salt, seeming to enjoy the brackish water. The thin-lipped grey mullet seems to like fresh water even more than the thick-lipped grey mullet.

Everyone knows what a *plaice* looks like with its orange spots; it is a common fish of sandy ground and can be caught in harbours and estuaries all year round. Plaice eat a lot of shellfish which is a good guide to what bait to provide for them.

Pouting, a species of small cod, has so many bones that some people call it pin-cushion fish; these make it so complicated to eat that many people refuse to bother with it, but it is all too easily caught when you are fishing for something better. It must be eaten absolutely fresh, for it goes off more quickly than any other fish. It turns up in estuaries and harbours during warmer weather, but does not on the whole like brackish water.

Salmon and sea trout, which in spite of spending the greater part of their lives in the sea, return to their native rivers to spawn.

Pollution and other factors have driven *sea trout* to the rivers of our west coast, and although some are taken along the coasts elsewhere, in nets, they will not enter the rivers if there is any pollution. Sea trout, unlike salmon, do feed in fresh water, and do not go so far offshore during the part of their lives they spend at sea. The sea trout is exactly the same fish as the ordinary brown trout, but no one has ever quite found out how or why some of the species decide to go to the sea and live consequently different lives. Sea trout move upriver from the spring through summer, but prefer hot clear settled weather in June to make their migrations.

Salmon, on the other hand, do not feed while in fresh water, begin to move upriver in early spring, in summer and autumn, and spawn during November and December, whereupon all but a few hen fish die. The small salmon or 'parr' spend a couple of years in the river and then migrate to the sea, where they stay for up to two years, growing fast, eventually to repeat the pattern. Salmon must have clean, well-oxygenated water, and have, like sea trout, been driven to the rivers which for the most part rise and run through hilly country. From Portsmouth, west, and right round Scotland and Ireland, the salmon run into the rivers. There was a time when salmon ran right up the Thames, but it is many a long year since that happened. Weirs and locks bar their way, although big efforts have been made to clean up the river downstream and careful checks are being kept on the fish that use it. Recently a salmon was taken which had managed to get quite a way up the river without being suffocated by pollution.

The sea and river *lamprey*, a parasitic but jawless fish, shaped like an eel, has a heavy toothed sucker with which it attaches itself to other fish and then exudes saliva which liquefies the muscles of the host. These rather unpleasant creatures, like the salmon, are spawned and reared in fresh water, and the young migrate to the sea. Adult sea lampreys return to estuaries in February and March to spawn upriver. Once considered to be a delicacy, and renowned as the cause of the death of Henry I who ate too many at a sitting, lampreys are not sought after these days. At one time river lampreys on migration were taken in their thousands and sold to the Dutch as bait, 400,000 fish per season being sold for forty shillings per thousand.

Eels abound in brackish water and muddy creeks and can be caught almost all year round in various ways (see page 126). Mature eels are believed to return to the Sargasso Sea where they mate and spawn, the young elvers returning in their millions to the rivers and streams of the world to grow to maturity. It is during these migrations that they can be caught in special eel traps set on weirs and other places which they must pass. (See pages 128 and 127 for recipes for cooking lampreys and eels.)

BAIT TABLE

Bass	Live sand eel, soft crab, live prawns, bits of kipper or bloater, bacon fat, lugworm or kingrag
Black Bream	Lugworm, kingrag, pounded-up crab, barnacles, herring strips, or boiled rice for ground bait
Cod, Haddock and Hake	Lugworm, crab, mussels, whelks or pieces of fish
Conger	Squid, cuttlefish, fresh mackerel or any other fish
Flounder	Worms, crabs, mussels, prawns or pieces of sand eel
Ling	Fresh whitebait
Grey Mullet	Breadpaste mixed with sugar, ragworm or fish guts
Mackerel	Bits of fish, sand eel or worms, or feathers or coloured wire on hooks for trolling with spinner
Plaice	Lugworm, ragworm, mussels or shrimps
Pollack	Sand eel, prawns or bits of herring

Skates and Rays	Chunks of fresh fish or sand eel
Sole	Worms or shrimps
Tope	Whole mackerel or herring, or any small whole fish
Tunny	Herring
Turbot	Live sand eel or worms
Whiting	Worms or pieces of mackerel
Wrasse	Live prawns or small bits of shellfish

Squid is very popular as a general bait because it is leathery and stays on the hook, and can be bought from most bait dealers who sell lugworms.

Seashore Fishing

Fishing from the shore, or from piers, one can catch almost all the fish mentioned in the last section, and several others besides. *Bass* like areas of low rock underwater and fast tideways, and the surf of sandy beaches when the sea is dropping after a gale, which is when surf

Black bream *(Basil M. Kidd)*

casters go after this species. They like both brackish and fresh water, and often choose a spot over sand where at low tide a freshwater stream runs to the sea. Best months for bass from the shore are May, June, September and October.

Cod which abound anywhere round Britain on any bottom from the end of October, through November and December can be caught from beaches and piers. The Norfolk, Suffolk, and Kent coasts provide specially good cod fishing.

As described above, *conger* may be taken almost anywhere where there are rocks or man-made crevices where they can lodge, specially in summer and autumn. *Dabs* abound on sandy beaches and estuaries. They are bottom feeders and can be caught almost anywhere in shallow water over sand. When shrimping with a push net over sand one frequently brings up baby dabs with the shrimps, and occasionally catches fish big enough to eat. They are at their best in the late summer and autumn. *Flounders* can be caught from piers and by fishing from the beach into calm water, and abound from March to November. *Garfish* can be caught from rocks and piers and from the shore in calm seas from early spring to late autumn and frequently run with the *mackerel* shoals. These follow the herring fry and whitebait and other small fish right inshore when they can be caught from the beach. This happens in June and right on through the summer, and in the warm south-western waters almost all year round. At times it is a dramatic sight. The shoals of thousands of small fish darken the water surface and splash as they try to escape the hunting mackerel, who themselves break the surface with mighty splashes. Above, the terns fly, and dive straight down to take the little fish. If you see a party of diving terns at a distance, it usually signifies a shoal of small fish and their attendant mackerel.

Grey mullet may be caught round rocks in calm weather. They like sheltered places, shallow water and calm seas, and can be found inshore from late March to late October. *Plaice* are also caught from the beach over sandy ground from spring to autumn. Small *pollack* can be caught from rocky beaches where they come in to feed, especially where there is a tide race, and can be found in some estuaries all year round. *Pouting* are caught from beaches and piers and almost any-where inshore from spring to autumn. There are several species of *skates* and *rays*. Thornback rays are taken sometimes from piers, or in shallow water by surf casting. The *sting ray* with its dangerous whip-like tail and venomous spine can inflict very unpleasant stings, and you should get medical help if stung. They come inshore in late summer and are caught from piers and beaches. All rays prefer muddy sand and gravelly bottoms to rocks.

Sole may be caught from shore or pier, mostly in summer, and night fishing often produces the best catches. *Whiting* abound during autumn and winter, and can be caught from shore or pier. The best whiting run on the east coast; west- and south-coast whiting are, for some reason, smaller. This member of the cod family makes good eating. *Wrasse* of several species frequent rocky shores and are fished for sport round our south and west coasts from April to October, but they make poor eating. *Tope* can be caught over sandy bottoms by surf casting during the summer months.

Boat Fishing

All the species mentioned in the last two sections may be caught from a boat using different fishing methods from those used from the shore. Some other species are normally only caught from boats. *Black bream* frequent certain offshore reefs off Bognor Regis and Littlehampton during spring and summer. *Haddock* can be caught round the Scottish

A good catch of turbot *(Basil M. Kidd)*

coast, and off north-east England and Ireland but are usually netted rather than fished for with rod and line. They abound in the autumn. *Ling* like deep water and a rocky bottom and are common off Scotland, Ireland and south Cornwall in the summer. Big *pollack* are to be found over rocky offshore reefs in fairly deep water where they appear in April and stay through the summer. *Tope* come inshore in spring and summer and like shallow channels and bays where the best specimens are caught from boats. The coast of Co Mayo in Ireland is noted for big *skate*. *Turbot* are the biggest and some say the tastiest flatfish. They like offshore sandbanks, such as the Varne off Folkestone or the skerries off the south coast, so one must go well out to sea to catch them. Turbot can be caught off the North Cornish coast all the year round.

Tunny fish can occasionally be caught off the Yorkshire coast, where they follow the herring shoals, as *mackerel* do the herring fry and whitebait. *Mackerel* can be caught during summer and autumn with almost any kind of rod or hand-line, with several hooks which bear feathers or have bits of coloured plastic-covered wire threaded on to them.

Netting

Seine netting either from the shore or from two boats is probably the easiest way to net fish, but can be hard and wet work. Basically a seine net is a long net, deep in the centre, which forms a wall, with cork floats at intervals along the top and lead weights along the bottom. Because it must be long enough to form a complete circle in the water, a seine net is an expensive piece of equipment.

One end of the net is held on shore, and the rest of the net, carefully folded, is placed in the stern of a boat which then rows out from the beach and back to it in a circle, paying out the net as it goes. The dinghy is then beached and both ends of the net are hauled in slowly and steadily, keeping the lower rope tauter than the upper one. This pulls the net well under the fish, and eventually all the catch is concentrated in a small area of the net and hauled clear of the sea.

A seine net used in deep water can obviously only catch surface fish, and quite a few will escape below the net.

A variation on seine netting is draw netting in which a single sheet of fine-mesh netting, with floats at the top and light weights at the bottom, is used in the edge of the sea. Two people at least are necessary for this operation – one on the inshore end of the net, and the other out

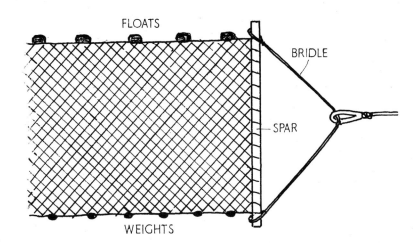

FLOATS

BRIDLE

SPAR

WEIGHTS

Seine netting

chest deep in the sea at the other end of the net. Both walk along parallel to the beach with the net stretched between them and when they feel the moment is ripe, the fisherman on the seaward end turns in towards the shore in a wide curve, while the one on the beach remains in position, and the net is then pulled round in exactly the same way as a seine net and both ends pulled up the beach. The number of people needed to work a draw net depends on its length and also on the weight of the catch. Several hands may be needed to bring the seaward

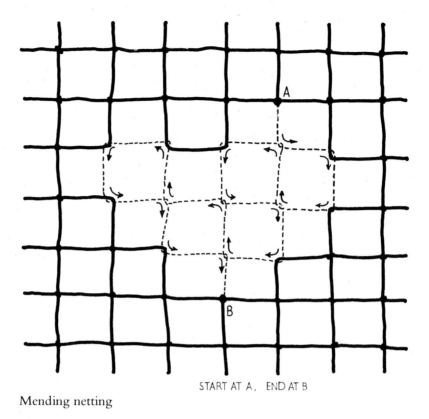

START AT A, END AT B

Mending netting

end ashore if there are plenty of fish in it; the catch can include cockles, crabs, plaice, flounders, sand eels, occasional soles and even bigger fish.

In some areas, such as the Chesil Beach in Dorset, when mullet shoal and swim down to the beach, watchers on shore pass the word along and the seine netters take one end of the nets out to sea in a boat and wait till the shoal arrives before encircling it back to the beach.

Nylon gill netting, which is fine and strong, has replaced the old type of hand-made and hand-mended net for drift netting, and for anchored sheet nets. It is cheaper to cut away old and torn nylon netting and replace it with new, than it is to spend days mending it mesh by mesh. Most netting of this type is done on a commercial basis, and does not really concern us here, but all kinds of crabs, crayfish, lobster, cod, pollack, rays, etc, can be caught in single sheets of this fine mesh, set with floats on the head rope, and pieces of chain to keep it down, and weights at the bottom ends or light anchors to hold the net in position.

Gill netting is hung to the head rope by means of short pieces of line

114

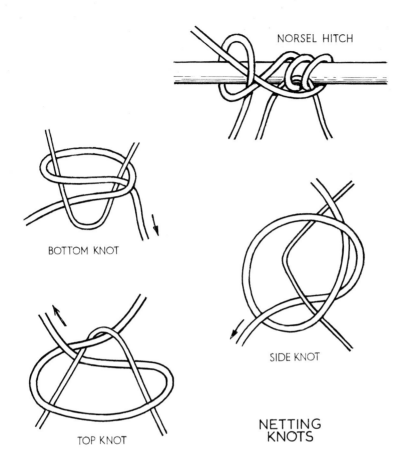

NETTING KNOTS

or 'norsels' attached to every fifth mesh point and tied to the head rope with a norsel hitch.

When joining pieces of net or mending nets the same basic knot is used, although it may start at a different point or lay in different directions. A netting needle is used and the trick is to match up mesh sizes; too small a mesh will cause the net to be drawn in and too big a mesh will make it baggy.

To mend a net, gather it up to a point about 3ft above the tear and hang it squarely so that you can handle the net and the needle evenly and make a good mend. Start at the highest point of the tear, working across as shown in the diagram, leaving the right-sized loops, and then down and across picking up the points of the loops as you go knotting and making the next row of loops.

To join a new piece of net, cut away the old torn net leaving a row of points, and then tie the new piece with side knots all the way down.

FURTHER READING   Piper, John. *All about Angling* (Pelham); Tryckare, T. and Cagner, E. *Fishing: The Complete Book* (David & Charles); Fletcher, D. *Pelham Manual for Sea Anglers* (Pelham); Gammon, C. *Sea Fishing* (Pelham); Walker, R. (ed) *The Shell Book of Angling* (David & Charles); Forbes, David Carl. *Successful Sea Angling* (David & Charles); *Teach Yourself Sea Angling* (English Universities Press); Judd, S. *Inshore Fishing* (Fishing News Books London Ltd); Wrangles, Alan (ed) *The Complete Guide to Sea Angling* (David & Charles); Wrangles and Tucker. *Sea Fishing for Fun* (David & Charles); Moriarty, C. *Eels* (David & Charles); Leakey, R. D. *Modern Inshore Fishing*; Lamb, Ted. *The Bait Book* (David & Charles).

EQUIPMENT   *Messrs R. & B. Leakey,* Belle Hill, Settle, Yorks BD24 0BB (all fishing tackle and inshore fishing gear, winches, pullers and line haulers, long lines, hooks, nets, and pots).

7

Food from Sea and Seashore, Fish and Shellfish

While many of the fish and shellfish dealt with in this chapter have been mentioned elsewhere in the book, I have for the sake of convenience put together details of how to harvest, prepare and cook all those which are not usually covered very fully in ordinary cookery books. Almost everyone knows how to deal with 'ordinary fish' when bought from a fishmonger; the fishmonger fillets it and cleans it, and every standard cookery book has whole sections of fish recipes. However it can be a very different matter when you are faced with a live crab or a bucketful of cockles or shrimps.

I doubt that many fishmongers have any idea how to clean lampreys, but it might so happen that some come your way if you live near an estuary.

Scallops and oysters have not been included, as scallops are deeper-water shellfish, not usually harvested inshore and are very much the prerogative of commercial fishermen; oysters are farmed commercially and are not just there for the finding.

There are a few plants from sea and seashore and cliff which are absolutely excellent, and which even locally, tend to be very neglected. Samphire, seakale and laverbread all have their local devotees and apart from being tasty and very good for you, laverbread in particular is a source of natural iodine. These are described in Chapter 15 with recipes.

Cooking Fresh Fish

Fish is at its best when it is absolutely fresh, for unless salted or frozen it goes off very quickly. Cod is a little wet when fresh (which is why it freezes so well) and some people like to keep it a day to dry out a little.

In the old days one used a fish kettle to cook big fish whole or in large pieces. These elongated steamers are rarely used these days. Clean the fish, place it on a large square of baking foil, season with salt and pepper and herbs according to recipes, and dot it with butter. Wrap it up in the foil so that no juices can escape, making a kind of envelope with all open edges folded upon themselves two or three times, and bake it in a shallow fireproof dish in a medium oven for about half an hour. Keep an eye on the oven heat and do not overcook. Open up and check that it has changed from a watery transparent substance to a flaky white opaque substance. Times are difficult to give because it depends upon the size of the fish. All juices are contained along with the cooking smells, so that other things can be cooked in the oven at the same time.

To serve the fish cold, unwrap it, and leave it to cool before removing it to a serving dish for garnishing. To serve hot, unwrap the fish and slide it on to a big dish complete with juices, which can then be drained off carefully to make stock for the appropriate sauce.

Fish steaks or pieces may be cooked in the same way to retain juices and flavour, and then finished off under a grill.

Dressing for Shellfish

A wonderful dressing for shellfish and indeed for any fish or salad may be made using lemon peel. Keep the outer husks of lemons that you use for other purposes in a polythene bag in the fridge so that they do not dry out. Scrape out as much of the white pith as possible, and discard it. Then liquidise the lemon peel with a little soda water or Perrier water. Add a little olive oil and salt and pepper to taste. This makes a very piquant emulsion of lemon peel. Experiment with the quantities of liquid and seasoning until you achieve a balance that you like.

Cockles

The edible cockle, *cardium edule,* inhabits tidal harbours and estuaries where there is sandy mud with a constant salinity. It is to be found in the middle and lower zones of the beach, but not up near high water mark. The shells are usually creamy white, occasionally bluish where the cockles live in mud. Each cockleshell consists of two equal hinged valves with many ribs. The cockle buries itself just under the surface and projects its two short siphons just above the sand. It draws in

Bagging up cockles at Brancaster

water through one siphon, extracts oxygen and the plankton and organisms on which it lives and then expels the water through the other siphon. Stand on cockle ground, and you will see these little spurts of water all over the place, giving a good clue to the whereabouts of the shellfish.

It is very easy to collect cockles, either by digging them out of the sand, or by using special cockle rakes with large teeth, for they are only just under the surface.

Where there are empty cockleshells, then there must be plenty of live ones not far away, for seagulls dig out cockles and then fly up to drop the shells on hard sand or rocks to open them, and starfish and several types of snail prey on them. In some areas there are huge beds of cockles which are literally farmed and sold commercially. 'Stiffkey Blues' are dug in the mudflats on the north Norfolk coast, near the village of that name, and at Brancaster there is a thriving industry. The cockles are washed and bagged and then kept under water in pounds until sold. The potting and preserving of cockles is another north Norfolk industry.

There are plenty of other large commercial beds, notably at Leigh-

119

on-Sea in the Thames estuary. In recent years there has been an outcry from cockle gatherers in South Wales that oyster catchers were eating so many cockles that the beds were being depleted. Consequently a misguided attempt was made to reduce the oyster catcher population by shooting them. Not surprisingly this had, if anything, an adverse effect on the cockle population. What had not been taken into account was that the oyster catchers also eat the snails which prey on the cockles and by killing the oyster catchers more snails lived to destroy the shellfish. There is, as always, a balance in these things, and man himself, by sheer greed and overcropping, is far more likely than anything else to upset that balance.

Cockles are a delicacy, but not if they are gritty, which they will be if not properly 'purged' and cooked. Give the shellfish a good wash in clean sea water and then put them in a bucket covered by fresh water and two handfuls of plain white flour or porridge oats. Swirl them round with your hand, and leave them overnight. The cockles will eat the flour and excrete along with most of it any sand and impurities they may have contained when you dug them. Next day, strain off the cockles and wash them thoroughly under a running tap. Drop them into a big pan, without further moisture, put on the lid and cook them gently for 4 or 5 minutes until the shells open. Throw away any shellfish which have not opened, and take out the flesh from the open shells. Eat the cockles immediately, at least on the same day.

Serve cockles in their shells with melted butter, or ready prepared and cold, out of their shells in small bowls with segments of lemon and brown buttered bread, salt, pepper and vinegar, so that the eater may take his choice. Many people prefer them this way to any other.

Cockles may be included in any mixed 'Fruits de Mer' recipe where mussels are specified and also make an excellent sauce for steamed, poached or boiled white fish.

Cockle Sauce

¼ pint cooked and prepared cockles	1 tsp lemon juice
½lb butter	salt and pepper

Melt the butter and add the other ingredients. If using salted butter be careful not to overdo the added salt. Serve very hot.

Cockle Pie

Collect about 100 cockles and prepare them as above. Chop the flesh with 4oz of previously fried bits of green bacon and 2 hard-boiled eggs. Sprinkle with a little cayenne papper. Butter an ovenproof dish and line it with mashed potato and fill it with the cockle mixture. Cover with more mashed potato and bake until nicely browned in a medium oven. Serve with wedges of lemon and a green vegetable.

Cockle Soup

2 quarts fresh cockles	1 pint milk
1½oz butter	small stick of chopped celery
1oz plain flour	2 tbsps chopped parsley
2 pints cockle liquid	salt and black pepper

Clean the cockles as above and boil them. Add up to a wineglassful of white wine if available. Strain the liquid and shell the cockles. Heat the butter and blend in the flour. Gradually add the liquid and milk, stirring all the time. Add the celery and salt and pepper. Simmer for 30 minutes. Add the cockles and parsley and simmer for a few more minutes before serving.

Mussels

The edible mussel, *mytilus edulis,* is to be found almost everywhere attached to rocks, breakwaters, piers, jetties, wrecks, in fact anything to which it can attach itself. When the Dutch set about getting rid of the Germans in 1944 they breached the dykes and flooded the island of Walcheren. A year later when the sea water was pumped out, the surface of the roads, the sides of the houses and even fences and branches of trees were found to be covered in mussels.

The mussel has a dark blackish blue shell and can vary enormously in size; it is roughly triangular in shape but elongated and with curved sides. The shells have two hinged valves which fit tightly. Mussels feed by opening their shells slightly and filtering out plankton, etc, from the sea water passing through.

Mussels are eaten in enormous quantities in Europe and especially in France, and their reputation for causing allergic illness, and stomach upsets, and even more serious infections is belied by the millions of Frenchmen who survive. Nevertheless mussels in polluted water do collect bacteria and other unpleasant substances and should not be collected from water which is obviously polluted, and in any case should be thoroughly cleansed by being kept in a bucket of either very clean sea water or fresh water with a handful of salt in it for at least 24 up to 48 hours. Cover the bucket with a cloth sprinkled with more salt and stand it in a cool place. Drain off the water, discard any broken or gaping mussels and any with shells which do not close properly or can be moved against each other, as these will be very gritty. Scrape off any sand, mud, limpets, and remove the beard or seaweedy part sticking out from the shell. Scrub them and wash them in several changes of water until there is no grit at the bottom of the bowl. Put them into a panful of water and boil them until they open. Discard any which do not open after 10 minutes. As an added precaution some cooks like to add a big pinch of bicarbonate of soda to the cooking water, but this can only be done if it is to be discarded and not used as the basis of a sauce.

Mussels release literally millions of eggs, up to 25 million from one mussel, at a single spawning. All mussels spawn during the full moon spring tides from June to September and the water becomes clouded with male sperm. Within six hours of fertilisation there are little larvae capable of swimming and there may be 170,000 swimming larvae beneath every square yard of water over the mussel bed. These will eventually after several changes, put out a byssus or thread and attach themselves to a fixed object where they can grow and feed as the tides rise and fall. French commercial mussel growers take advantage of this enormously prolific spawning habit by providing hurdle fences set on deeply embedded posts out on the mudflats of such places as the bay of Mont St Michel. The mussels are harvested carefully when they reach the required size, and always enough are left to grow on and to restock the beds. The harvested mussels are thoroughly washed in strong jets of pumped clean sea water, before being graded and sold.

There is no reason why, should you be able to set up a hurdle on posts, in a place where there are already wild mussels, and provided that there is a good flow of water, and that it is unpolluted, you should not eventually harvest your own mussels. Obviously the fences need to be pretty strong because mussels thrive in fast-moving water, and rough seas will soon flatten anything which is not well bedded in or which presents too solid a resistance to the water. Sheep hurdles on good long posts should do the trick.

Moules Marinière

Allow about 1½ pints of mussels per person and prepare them as above, but to every 2 pints of water add one large glass of dry white wine or cider, and as soon as they are open put them in a warmed bowl. When they are all ready, strain the liquid through a cloth, boil it again quickly and pour it over the mussels, adding a little chopped parsley. Serve with French bread, in soup plates, with a fork plus a soup spoon for the liquid and a large extra bowl for the empty shells.

This is a very basic recipe and the French add a couple of cloves of garlic to the liquid which makes it quite delicious if you like garlic.

Special Moules Marinière

1½ pints mussels
4 shallots
1 tbsp butter
½ pint dry white wine
2 sprigs thyme
2 tbsps chopped parsley
1 bay leaf

For the Roux
2 tbsps butter
1 tbsp plain flour
black pepper

Chop the shallots finely and fry them gently in the butter, and add the wine, thyme, parsley and bay leaf. Cook the cleaned mussels in this and when opened, remove them and boil the liquid very quickly until it is reduced by half. Thicken it by making a roux with the butter and flour, adding the liquid slowly, stirring all the time. Season with black pepper, pour it over the mussels, and sprinkle on a little more parsley.

Cream of Mussel Soup

2lb mussels
2 glasses white wine
2 chopped onions
1 clove garlic, chopped
1 sprig parsley
½ tsp thyme

salt and black pepper
cayene pepper
1 bay leaf
2oz butter
1 egg yolk
1 large carton double cream

Clean the mussels as above and combine them with the wine, onions and garlic, parsley, thyme, salt and pepper to taste, a sprinkle of cayenne pepper, the bay leaf and butter. Cover the pan and cook until the mussels have opened. Remove the mussels, discarding any which have not opened and simmer the liquid for another 10 minutes while you remove the mussels from their shells. Strain the liquid carefully. Beat the egg yolk and cream and add them slowly to the mussel liquid and cook until it has thickened, but do not let it boil. Add the mussels just before serving. This soup can be eaten either hot or cold.

Mussel Pilau

2 quarts mussels
¼ cup olive oil
1 chopped onion
1 glass white wine

1½ pints light chicken stock
salt and pepper
½lb long grain rice
grated cheese

Prepare the mussels as above and then heat the oil, add the onion and fry it until golden. Add the mussels, stir them round a bit and then leave them until they open, then add the wine, stock and salt and pepper. Bring to the boil and then simmer for about 10 minutes. Take out the mussels and discard any unopened ones. Wash the rice in a sieve under cold water for a few minutes to get rid of some of the starch, and then add it to the mussel liquid. Cook until the rice is nearly done and add the shelled mussels and cook gently until all the liquid is absorbed and the rice tender. Sprinkle with a little grated cheese.

Mussel Stew

2 quarts mussels
½ bottle white wine
2 tbsps butter
2 tbsps plain flour
1 pint milk

2 minced onions
1 clove garlic, pressed
salt and black pepper
2 tbsps chopped parsley
½ pint single cream

Prepare the mussels as above, then put them in a saucepan with the wine and let them simmer for about 10 minutes until they are open. Strain the liquid and remove the mussels from their shells. Melt the butter and make a roux with the flour, add the liquor and the milk slowly, stirring all the time. Add the onions and garlic and simmer for 10 minutes. Add salt and pepper to taste, with the mussels, chopped parsley and cream. Heat through, but do not let it boil again, as the mussels might become rather tough and rubbery. Serve it very hot with plenty of hot French bread.

Norfolk Mussel Pudding

2 pints mussels
½lb SR flour
3oz shredded suet

pinch of salt
salt and pepper

Make the suet crust with the flour, suet, pinch of salt and water, and roll it out. Put it on a piece of greased greaseproof paper. Prepare the mussels as above and put them in boiling water until they open.

Remove them from their shells, put them in the dough, season with salt and pepper. Tie up the dough in a cloth and steam it for 1½ hours.

(Mary Norwak)

Whelks

The common whelk, *buccinum undatum,* is not found in the tidal zones of the beach, but further out to sea. Whelks are caught by setting pots for them, and this is a very simple matter. Any old bucket or can with an open top will do. It must be weighted with stones or heavy metal so that it will rest on the sea bed and the open top should be covered with a piece of netting with a hole in it big enough for the whelks to crawl through. The pot is baited with fish offal put in the bottom, the net securely tied and it is then dropped to the sea bottom on a buoyed line. A 1-gallon polythene bottle, securely sealed, makes a good marker, and be sure that you allow enough line so that the marker is not pulled under water at high tide. A small dan or float buoy will do just as well, or you may prefer a stick with a flag on it passed through several pieces of cork. The marker should be clearly visible especially if the pot is being set anywhere where fishing boats may pass. You will not be at all popular if your whelk pot line fouls somebody's propeller, or is situated just where they habitually trawl for fish.

Check the pot daily and you will find that quite a few whelks have crawled in to get at the bait. Remove the catch, rebait the pot and reset it.

Make sure that the whelks you have are the edible type, by checking against the plates in a book such as *The Observer's Book of Sea and Seashore.* The edible whelk is the biggest of our species, several inches high and with deep grooves. The shell is creamyish yellow, especially round the open mouth area.

To Cook Whelks

First wash them thoroughly in two or three lots of clean sea water. Some people like to purge them in the same way as cockles by leaving them overnight in a bucket of water with a handful of plain flour or oatmeal.

Put the whelks into boiling water, bring them back to the boil and cook for 15 to 20 minutes, until the operculum or 'scab' begins to come away. Drain, remove from the shells and eat very fresh with vinegar, pepper, lemon juice and brown bread. If whelks are boiled for too long they go black and look most unappetising. Whelks are at their best during the summer months which has made them a popular seaside treat for many people.

Winkles

The edible winkle, *littorina littorea,* is usually a dark greenish-greyish black, and can grow as big as 1in long. Occasionally winkles are brown or reddish with darker concentric lines. The shell is rounded and has a few coils up to a sharp apex. It is found absolutely everywhere, exposed as the tide goes out. Always gather winkles from clean rocks and rock pools.

To Cook Winkles
Wash the winkles well and then put them in a large pan, cover with water and bring to the boil. Cook them for 5 minutes before draining them. The recipe below suggests using some of the water they were boiled in for making the soup, but be careful to scoop the liquid from the top or else strain it very carefully through fine muslin or it will be gritty. Take the winkles out of the shells with a long needle or pin.

Winkle Soup
Prepare the winkles as above, and pour about $\frac{3}{4}$ pint of the liquid they were cooked in into a clean saucepan with an equal amount of fresh water or water and milk. Bring it to the boil and add, very slowly, enough oatmeal to make it the consistency of thin gruel. Cook the oatmeal for about 20 minutes, then put the winkles into it and cook for another 10 minutes. Add seasoning and serve very hot.

Eels

Eels make excellent eating, and are easy to catch. Perhaps it is their snake-like looks and tendency to wriggle and die slowly which puts people off them. Eels can be caught in 'hives', torpedo-like withy baskets which are baited with such things as fresh chicken guts, or shrimp heads, or almost any fresh meat or fishy waste. Fine-mesh wire cages do the same job perfectly well. These are sunk below the water surface and left overnight. Fyke nets are specially useful in estuaries where they can be staked down so that the fish cannot pass beneath them. They consist of a kind of net wall, a leader net which guides the eels into the funnel-shaped 'fyke' set with the narrow end towards deep water. The net encloses a series of funnels through which the eels

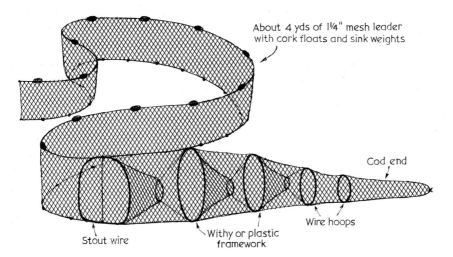

About 4 yds of 1¼" mesh leader with cork floats and sink weights

Cod end

Wire hoops

Stout wire

Withy or plastic framework

Fyke net for migrating eels: this type of eel net, 2.2 metres long, is staked down in shallow places where migrating eels cannot pass it. The fish are diverted into the trap by the leader net. The net is set with the cod-end towards deep waters

cannot return. Mature eels return to the sea after seven or eight years to swim off to the Sargasso Sea to mate, and it is these big fish (the best for smoking) which can be trapped on weirs which they have to negotiate to reach the sea. Another method is to bait a longline (see page 102) with earthworms and leave it in the water overnight. Eels can also be caught by 'babbing', that is by tying a bunch of worms, each threaded on to knitting wool, on the end of a piece of string on a stick. Lower this to the bottom of the stream or in a shallow estuary and after a few minutes bring it up and shake off the eels that are clinging to it.

To Smoke Eels

Gut but do not skin them. Clean them and lay them in dry salt for 12 hours. Hang them on a stick and dip into boiling water for a few seconds to open the fish out. Smoke at 140°F (60°C) for 2 to 4 hours, according to size. (See also page 141 on Home Smoking.)

Jellied Eels

2lb eels
2 pints cold water
1 large onion, chopped
1 bay leaf and sprig parsley

1 tbsp vinegar
salt and pepper
whites and crushed shells of 2 eggs
2oz gelatine

127

Clean and skin the eels and put them into a pan with the water and all the other ingredients except the eggs and gelatine. Simmer for about 15 minutes until the eels are tender. Take out the fish, cut them into pieces and remove the bones. Strain the liquid and return it to the pan with the egg shells and lightly whisked whites of the eggs. Add the gelatine, mixed according to the instructions on the packet, and bring to the boil. Simmer for 2 minutes and then strain it again. Line a bowl with the pieces of eel, add the jelly and leave it to set.

Eel pie

Clean, skin and cut 1¾lb eels into pieces 2in long. Dry each piece, placing a piece of butter inside with a little pepper, salt and chopped parsley. Lay them in a pie dish with a cupful of vinegar and water mixed. Thicken with a teaspoon of plain flour. Cover with a good puff pastry, and bake in a hot oven. Serve cold.

(Mary Norwak)

Lampreys

Medium-sized lampreys are the best for eating, especially those caught in the mouths of rivers. The flesh is delicate but rather fatty, and some people find it a bit indigestible.

Prepare the fish by scalding it (dip it in boiling water) so that the skin can be peeled off easily. Then take out the central nerve: cut off the tip of the lamprey's tail, make an incision round the neck below the gills and through this incision, catch hold of the nerve and pull it out. Slit and clean the fish.

Lampreys en Matelote

Chop 1lb of prepared lamprey into 2in pieces and put them into a pint of boiling red wine and simmer for about an hour. Make a roux with butter and flour and add the wine to it gradually, stirring all the time. Season to taste.

Stuffed Lamprey

1 medium-sized lamprey
suet forcemeat (parsley and
    thyme stuffing)
butter
1 beaten egg

breadcrumbs
1 lemon
anchovy sauce
salt and black pepper

128

Prepare the lamprey as above, fill the body with the stuffing and sew it up. Butter some greaseproof paper or kitchen foil and wrap the fish up in it. Cover with hot water and simmer for 20 minutes. Drain and dry the fish. Melt some butter in a baking dish and put the lamprey in it. Brush it with the beaten egg and coat with breadcrumbs and bake in a medium oven for about 30 minutes, by which time it should be nicely browned. Serve with lemon, anchovy sauce, salt and black pepper.

Prawns and Shrimps

The large and succulent prawn may be caught in rock pools all round our coast. The prawn is carnivorous and is attracted instantly to raw fish, raw meat, or such tasty and highly smelling things as pieces of kipper, so these are used to bait prawn nets. The most successful type of prawn net is the drop net used in pools and gullies in the rocks at low tide. The net consists of a circular hoop of metal about a foot in diameter with a cone-shaped fine-mesh net bag beneath it. Above the hoop the net is attached by three lines to a cork float, and through that to another cork float (both about 4in by 4in by 2in, with edges rounded with a wood file so that they do not crumble) set at the exact depth of the water in the pool being fished. The top float should be painted white so that it can easily be picked out at night. The net is dropped into the pool and the lower float lifts the hoop just clear of the bottom to make a bag; the fisherman retreats and allows some time for the prawns to go for the bait, then, quietly he reaches forward, grabs the top float and lifts the whole contraption clear of the water. The trick is to strike quickly so that the very nervous prawns have no time to dart back out of the net. Sometimes it is necessary to use a long pole to lift the net out of the water. This type of prawn fishing, using several nets, can be done at low tide in calm weather from a boat in shallow water over the rocks, or on foot among the rocks. Some prawners prefer to work at night.

Shrimping is done quite differently. Shrimps are present in their millions along the water's edge over many sandy and slightly muddy shores. Use a push net, as wide as you have the strength to work, exactly the same shape as but much bigger than a child's shrimping net. You shove it along the bottom in anything up to waist-deep water. Unless the sea is warm, this must be done wearing thigh boots and is always an exhausting and wet job. Every few yards the net must be lifted out of the water, and the catch, which may include small flatfish and sand eels, must be transferred to a carrying bag or bucket

129

Prawn net

slung round your waist. The shrimp net consists of a stout pole attached to a piece of flat wood which is shaped below so that it will slide along the sand and not dig in. This is braced back to the pole with a wooden or metal hoop, and between the two is attached a net so as to form a shallow bag. Further bracing may be necessary if the net is wide. A net with a 4ft leader board is enough for most people, but professional shrimpers work with nets up to 5 or 6ft wide.

In the South West, rock prawn cube traps are used. These are quite small and when baited with the flesh of shore crabs which crawl into them – this discourages others from doing the same – should catch many prawns which get in and cannot get out.

All the following recipes may be made with prawns instead of shrimps, and good-sized prawns if you are lucky enough to catch them, may be used for scampi. If possible cook shrimps in sea water which has been strained through a fine muslin cloth, but if you are in any doubt as to the cleanliness of the sea in your area, put the live shrimps into boiling fresh water with salt and no other seasoning. The more salt the pinker the shrimps.

Greek Shrimps

2lb unpeeled shrimps
¼ cup olive oil
2 chopped onions
1 tbsp tomato purée

4 peeled and chopped
    tomatoes
2 tbsps chopped parsley
salt and pepper

Wash the shrimps and drain them. Heat the oil and fry the onions in it for about 5 minutes, then add the purée and the tomatoes and cook for another 5 minutes. Add the parsley, salt, pepper and the shrimps. Cover the pan and cook for 15 minutes. Scoop the pink shrimps from the oil and remove the heads and shells. Return them to the oil, onion and tomato mixture, reheat and serve on a bed of rice.

Shrimp Sauce

½ pint shrimps
½ pint white sauce
1 tsp anchovy essence

few drops of lemon juice
dash of cayenne pepper

Prepare the shrimps as above and shell them. Boil the shells and heads in an equal amount of milk and water for 5 minutes to make stock for the white sauce, as this will give more flavour. Strain, make the white sauce, add the shrimps, anchovy essence, lemon juice and cayenne. Let it heat for a few minutes, but do not boil. Serve with plain white fish.

Shrimp Rarebit

½ pint cleaned shrimps
4oz grated cheese
½ cup milk
pinch of cayene pepper

salt
1 dssrtsp Worcestershire sauce
1 beaten egg
toast

Melt the cheese in the milk, add the seasonings and Worcestershire sauce. Then add the shrimps and simmer till they are heated through. Remove from the heat and add the egg. Reheat till the mixture thickens, but do not boil it. Make pieces of toast and butter them, then pour the mixture over the toast. Put them under the grill until the mixture bubbles and the top is browned.

Devilled Shrimps

1lb shelled shrimps
½ cup dry white wine

salt
pinch of thyme

131

1 tbsp brandy	1 bay leaf
1 sliced carrot	1 tbsp double cream
1 small sliced onion	1 tbsp dry sherry
1 sprig parsley	$\frac{1}{2}$ cup home-made mayonnaise
1 clove garlic, pressed	1 dozen pitted olives

Combine the wine, brandy, carrot, onion, parsley, garlic, salt, thyme and bay leaf, bring to the boil and add the shrimps, and simmer for about 10 minutes. Let it cool, then scoop out the shrimps. Blend the cream and sherry with the mayonnaise, and add the chopped olives. Put the shrimps on a plate and cover with mayonnaise mixture and chill thoroughly before serving.

The liquid in which the shrimps were cooked is far too good to be thrown away. Make a roux with butter, flour and milk, and add the strained liquid to it, add a few chopped shrimps and serve as soup with croûtons of bread.

Shrimp Paste

$\frac{1}{2}$lb cooked shrimps	1 tsp anchovy essence
$\frac{1}{2}$lb boned and skinned cod	pinch of cayenne pepper
or other white fish	pinch of mace
lemon juice	6oz butter

Shell the cooked shrimps, and then save the shells and heads and boil them in just enough water to cover them, for 30 minutes. Strain this liquid and cook the white fish in it for 10 minutes. Drain the fish, but leave just a little of the liquid with it and break it up thoroughly with a fork. Add the lemon juice, anchovy essence, cayenne and mace to taste. When it is quite cold add 5oz of butter and beat it until it is quite smooth, then add the chopped shrimps, and heat everything slightly. Press it into a suitably sized pot or jar, leave to cool again, melt the last ounce of butter and pour this over the top to seal the paste. Keep in the fridge and serve on brown bread and butter.

Shrimp de Jonghe

1lb cleaned shrimps	2 slices bread
2 tbsps white wine	2 tbsps chopped leek
pepper	1 clove garlic, pressed
1oz butter	salt

Put the shrimps in a fireproof dish, add the wine and pepper, dot with butter. Make the bread into crumbs and add the leek, garlic and salt, and mix thoroughly. Spread this over the shrimps and bake in a moderate oven for 20 minutes.

Handling Lobsters and Crabs

Lobsters can inflict a hefty nip with those fearsome claws, and big crabs can grip quite hard. However, neither creature can reach backwards, and lobsters should be held firmly round the body well behind the claws. Crabs should be picked up from the rear with the hand grasping above and below the body. Small crabs, rock crabs, etc, which can be spanned by the hand, can be picked up safely with thumb and middle finger, one each side of the shell just behind the serrated edge of the top shell.

Crab and lobster fishermen snick the claw tendon in the first joint with a knife and tie the claws shut with a piece of string if the creatures are to be stored together live in boxes or in pounds before being sold. Like all types of fishing there are some unpleasant aspects but if you wish to catch and eat your own crabs and lobsters, then there is no place for squeamishness.

By the way, should you catch a conger in a lobster or crab pot, detach the pot from the back line and tow it home behind your boat to get rid of the smell of the eel, otherwise crabs and lobsters will not enter the pot.

Lobsters

Unfortunately the common lobster, *homarus vulgaris,* has become rare due to over-fishing, in spite of minimum size regulations. Lobsters live in rocky places and only reach a density of about ten per acre, and are easy prey for the skin diver, which has not helped their chances wherever the water is fairly clear. However, there are still plenty of lobsters in deeper water to keep the species going, and still some to be caught inshore where there are rocks and seaweed. Lobsters crawl into holes and crevices, sometimes backwards, and it is this habit which makes them easy to catch in pots. The traditional lobster pot is a large circular net basket with a heavy base and a funnel-shaped hole in the top, but almost any kind of framework covered with netting with a funnel-shaped hole in it will catch lobsters (and edible crabs, see page 138). The pots must be baited with fish offal, soft crabs or fish pieces, almost anything will attract them. Commercial fishermen put out pots singly where the bottom is extremely rocky and uneven, or in multiples joined together by a back line so that they can be hauled one

Mending a lobster pot: note netting knots

after the other, where the bottom is fairly smooth and not likely to cause pots to become jammed.

The pot in the photograph is made of four heavy pieces of iron piping, lashed together at the corners, and hoops made of iron rods, also lashed to the framework. The dimensions of the base are about 28 × 18in and the height is about 18in. Each end of the pot is made of netting woven smaller and smaller to make a funnel, ending in a ring of rope about $4\frac{1}{2}$in in diameter. The bottom is $\frac{1}{2}$in wire netting. The top and sides are netting, with a flap on one half of one side which can be opened to bait the pot and remove the catch. Inside the pot are a couple of taut strings, knotted so as to be double for a few inches, into which tight loop the bait can be pushed and will remain suspended in the middle of the pot.

The netting is hand made of rough, hairy, hemp string, but this can be any suitable strong netting twine. The pot is attached to a rope by means of a bridle to the hoops at each end. At the top end of the rope is a plastic bottle as a float, and then a couple or three yards of twine leading to a cork buoy and flag.

Much bigger wooden 'pots' are favoured in some areas. These are merely oblong boxes made of battening, bolted together and then covered with netting, having the same funnel arrangement at each end or at one end through which the lobsters pass to get at the bait suspended inside, only to be unable to get out again.

Some of these long pots have an extra compartment with a funnel through which the lobster can pass into a 'parlour', a kind of holding pen. I have seen these interior funnels made of pieces of plastic fencing, rolled round to make a tube, with a hinged flap at the inner end, rather like a garden fork, made of pieces of wire soldered together. The idea being that the lobster can push through into the pen, but cannot return or drive the other lobsters away from the pot entrance. Both crab and lobster pots can be bought which are made of plastic netting, and are collapsible and stackable. Their advocates claim that they save time and effort because they are lighter to handle and easier to work from a boat, and that they collapse under extreme wave pressure rather than bump along the sea bottom and break as traditional pots may do.

Pots should be visited daily and checked, or where lobsters are plentiful, raised and rebaited several times during the course of a morning's fishing. Usually there will be small rock crabs in the pot, which can be removed from their shells and used to rebait the pot. Small edible crabs (see page 138) may also have found their way in, but should be returned to the sea unless they are at least $4\frac{1}{2}$in across, as should all lobsters below $10\frac{1}{2}$in in length. Crab and lobster fishermen carry wood measures at minimum size with which they can instantly measure doubtful specimens.

On the south and west coasts the rock lobster or crawfish, *palinurus eliphas,* may also be caught in pots.

To Cook Lobster

There are two schools of thought about boiling a lobster. One says it is more humane to plunge it into boiling water head first, and the other put it into cold water and slowly bring it to the boil. Both ways are pretty unpleasant, but if you want to eat lobster, it has to be done.

When the lobster is in the pot, bring the water back to the boil, cover, and leave it to cook for 20 minutes, or a little more if it is a big one. Do not overcook or the flesh will become soft and stringy.

Pull off the small claws and pick out the meat. Crack the big claws, removing the meat if required, or leaving it in if the lobster is to be served cold in its shell. Split the tail right down with a sharp knife, and the body, being careful not to break the stomach, a small sac just behind the head. Remove all traces of the intestinal canal which shows as a dark thread down the tail. Throw away the spongy tissue which

135

lies between the meat and the shell. Remove the intestinal cord from the body also, and remove the stomach if the shell is to be used to hold the meat. Keep any bright red coral, and the green liver, for sauce or garnish.

Lobster Thermidor

1 boiled lobster
2 tbsps butter
1 small onion, minced
pinch of cayenne pepper
1 glass dry white wine

½lb chopped mushrooms
1 tbsp tomato purée
¼ pint white sauce
2oz grated cheese

Take all the meat off the lobster and cut it up small. Heat the butter and gently fry the onion in it until it is just golden, then add the lobster pieces, cayenne pepper and white wine. Cook for 5 minutes and add the chopped mushrooms and tomato purée. Cook this for a few more minutes and then put it into the lobster shells, on a flat oven dish. Pour the white sauce over, sprinkle with the grated cheese and bake for a few minutes in a hot oven. Brown the cheese under a hot grill and serve very hot.

Lobster Newburg

1lb cooked lobster meat
4 tbsps butter
4 tsps brandy
2 egg yolks, beaten

½ pint double cream
salt and black pepper
cayenne pepper
paprika pepper

Chop the lobster meat and fry it gently in the butter, add the warmed brandy and flame it. Stir the egg yolks into the cream and put this into a double saucepan. Heat without boiling, stirring all the time, until it has thickened. Add the lobster and pan juices, and heat again. Add the salt, pepper, cayenne and paprika to taste, and serve on rice or in vol-au-vent cases.

Lobster and Avocado Salad

1 lobster
¼ cucumber
2 hard-boiled eggs

salt and black pepper
dash of cayenne pepper
tarragon

(Opposite) Lobster pot: note entrance and bridle

2 avocado pears   chives
juice of 1 lemon   parsley
$\frac{1}{4}$ pint home-made mayonnaise

Cut the lobster, cucumber and hard-boiled eggs into small cubes. Cut the avocados in half and scoop out the flesh as neatly as possible, then cut it into cubes. Cover these with lemon juice, and also sprinkle a little juice inside the avocado skins. Mix the diced lobster, eggs, cucumber and avocado in a bowl and add the mayonnaise, with salt, pepper and cayenne to taste. Put this carefully back into the avocado skins and garnish with chopped tarragon, chives and parsley. Chill before serving.

Crabs

The edible crab, *cancer pagurus*, lives in deep water, but it is always worth looking under rocks and stones down near the water's edge at low spring tides. However, most crabs are caught by setting pots for them, and as they can be found almost anywhere on sandy or rocky shores, even where the rocks are minimal, plenty are caught, especially during the summer months when pots can be set without risk of loss in rough seas. Crabs travel in search of food which makes them easier to catch than lobsters.

Crab pots differ from the lobster pots described above, in that they have a single wide netting funnel running from one side of the pot to the other, with a hole in the middle so that the crabs can drop down into the body of the pot where the bait is suspended in its double string. Of approximately the same dimensions and construction as the lobster pot (see page 133), the crab pot usually has four hoops, either of iron or wood. The funnel is set between the two central hoops. A flap of netting with a rod at the bottom end, which can be securely tied or hooked down, makes it easier to get at the catch and to rebait the pot.

Leakey's folding traps which are easy to shoot, and to free if caught in rocks, collapse under severe wave pressure, so do not suffer the rolling and tumbling on the sea bottom which ruins non-collapsible traps. These pots are attached by means of a short line with a toggle at the top of the hoop on the rear end to a 12in line with a loop in the end, itself attached to the back line carrying all the pots at up to 10-fathom intervals. Thus the pot can be quickly attached to and detached from the back line while fishing, and folds after servicing and closing in the boat. The back line loops are dropped over a conveniently placed vertical stick and the pots reattached by their toggles as the line is shot again.

138

Float and buoy for any
kind of fishing pot

To Cook Crab

Put the crab into cold water and slowly bring it to the boil. Boil for 20
minutes and leave it to get cool before preparing it. If a crab is missing
a claw, stuff some bread in the hole otherwise the meat will become
waterlogged during cooking.

Dressed Crab

Place the cooked crab on its back with the tail flap towards you.
Remove the claws and legs by twisting them inwards. Then separate
the body from the shell by putting your thumbs under the tail flap and
pushing upwards until the body breaks away from the shell. Remove
the mouth and stomach bag by turning the crab so that the mouth
faces you and press your thumbs down and forward on the mouth
until this and the stomach bag break away with a click. Throw them
both away. Then loosen all the soft brown meat (or coral) round the

Sheringham longshoremen hauling up their crabber. The tallest man wears thigh boots, serge trousers, and a Guernsey under his smock

inside of the shell with the handle of a spoon, and put it in a bowl. Next trim the shell by tapping round the shell cavity with a knife handle and pressing with your thumbs until the edges of the shell wall break away neatly. Wash the shell under the tap and dry it. Take the body of the crab and discard the 'white men's fingers'. Scrape off any remaining brown meat and add it to the rest of the bowl. In a separate bowl put the white meat from the legs and claws. Nutcrackers gently used along the claws, just to crack the shell which can then be picked away is probably the easiest and least messy way to get the meat out.

There are many ways to finish off the crab meat and dressed crabs bought from a fishmonger look very nice, but often have bread-crumbs added to the red meat to add bulk. Season the red meat with a few drops of olive oil and a little lemon juice or vinegar, salt and pepper. Shred the white meat separately, season that a little and arrange both meats in the empty shell. Sprinkle with the sieved yolk of a hard-boiled egg and the chopped white over the top and garnish with chopped parsley.

Crabmeat Casserole

1 crab
2oz butter
2 tbsps plain flour
$\frac{1}{2}$ pint milk
$\frac{1}{2}$lb grated cheese

$\frac{1}{4}$lb chopped mushrooms
1 chopped green pepper
salt and pepper
pinch of cayenne pepper
flaky pastry or breadcrumbs

140

Prepare the crab as above and take all the meat from it, but mix the coral and white together. Make a roux with the butter and flour, add the milk slowly and cook for a few minutes. Add the cheese, stir again, and then add all the other ingredients, except the pastry or breadcrumbs, and mix them well. Put this into a shallow ovenproof dish, cover with pastry and bake in a moderate oven for about 30 minutes. If breadcrumbs are used, put a few dabs of butter on the top and sprinkle with cayenne pepper.

Crab Newburg

1 crab	1 tbsp sherry
2oz butter	2 egg yolks
salt and cayenne pepper	$\frac{1}{4}$ pint cream

Prepare the crab and take all the meat from it as above, but mix the white and coral together. Cook this meat in the butter for about 5 minutes, then add the seasonings and sherry. Blend the egg yolks and cream. Remove the crab from the stove and add the egg mixture. Reheat in a double saucepan, till it thickens, but do not let it boil. Serve on hot buttered toast or muffins.

Home Smoking

Small home smokers which take just a few fish or pieces of bacon, sausages or poultry, come in several sizes and are most convenient if you just wish to do small quantities at a time for fairly immediate consumption. These can be bought at good kitchen utensil shops.

'Salmon King' smokers which take about 30 herrings or 8 salmon sides are made of enamelled steel and have the necessary smoking compartment, racks, hooks and smoke generator housing, and cold smoke fish and other food slowly but extremely effectively using wood shavings and smoking powder. The Swedish 'Barracuda' cold smoker takes about 16lb of fish and does the job in 45 minutes. The small North American model holds about 7lb of fish and will hot or cold smoke. The wood shavings in all three models are ignited by solid fuel soaked in meths, meths briquettes or, in the Swedish model, charcoal.

To set up a smoke house on a big scale for cold smoking you need a small wooden hut like a 'privy' with a concrete floor, and a wire-netting rack inside about 4ft from the floor on which to lay the

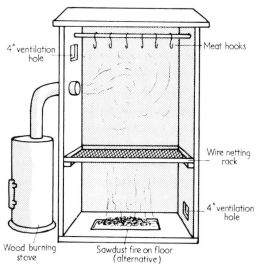

4" ventilation hole

Meat hooks

Wire netting rack

4" ventilation hole

Wood burning stove

Sawdust fire on floor (alternative)

A simple smoke-house

produce, and a woodburning stove. This can be set up just outside the hut with a chimney directly into it, so that cool smoke fills the hut. A woodburning stove inside the house can be used to provide smoke for the hut set up against the outside wall. If hotter smoke is needed then a fire can be lit on the floor of the smoker using wood chips and sawdust. In this case two ventilation holes must be made to create enough draught to make the fire burn. Each should be 4 to 6in square with sliding flaps. One should be at floor level, and the other high up on the opposite side. Once the fire has been lit, adjust the flaps until it is smouldering but not blazing.

The sawdust should preferably be from hardwood, with some oak in it. Two bucketfuls per twenty-four hours should be enough. A little birch sawdust and some fir cones improve the flavour of the fish. Light a twist of paper and feed sawdust on to it in a heap till the smoke is rising nicely. Keep an eye on it to see that it remains alight but does not burn away too quickly.

Cold smoking means that the temperature on the surface of the food being smoked should not go above 120°F (50°C). Between 100° and 110°F (39° and 43°C) is ideal. Hot smoking from 150° to 200°F (65° to 93°C) cooks the food as well as smokes it, but it must be eaten within a few days. In America and Germany hot smoking is common and the beautiful smoked bacon, etc, which one slices thinly and eats without further cooking is done this way.

142

The following recipe describes a standard method of smoking fish. Clean and bone haddock and sprinkle it with rock salt. After 12 hours wash and dry it with a cloth and hang it up to dry for 2 or 3 hours, then lay it on the rack to smoke. The fish should be nicely smoked in 12 hours. Be sure the smoke is not too hot or it will cook the fish rather than smoke it. Once the fish is smoked bring it indoors into a warm room to dry off properly before wrapping it in greaseproof paper for keeping in the fridge. Smoked fish can be deep-frozen.

Fish which are to be eaten within a few days of smoking need not be over-preserved. Put them straight into a brine bath of rock salt with twice its volume of water. Herrings, trout and flatfish go into this bath without being cleaned and are left for about 5 hours before being taken out and cleaned and hung up to drain for a few more hours before being smoked. Fish which have been cleaned should only be left in the brine solution for at most 1½ hours as they will quickly absorb the salt.

Herrings for kippers are split and cleaned, put into brine as above for 30 minutes, hung up to dry and then smoked for about 8 hours.

All commercially smoked fish absorbs its bright colour from dye which is added to the brine. Home-smoked fish does not look so vivid, but will probably taste much better!

Conservation and Pollution

All these delicious fruits of the sea are endangered by pollution from time to time. I am not a conservationist for conservation's sake. Thoughtlessly to support every conservation cause just because someone is trying to build something or to do something where nothing has been built or done before is ridiculous. All creatures, including man, are entitled to the use of their habitat, and I believe that everyone has an equal right to access to sea, seashore, and river, provided he respects established rights of property, and perpetrates no vandalism in its widest sense. Unfortunately unlike the other creatures on our planet, man must make buildings for shelter, must make roads for access, must have available the supplies he needs to buy in order to live, must have public conveniences, must have camping sites, and must produce an enormous amount of rubbish. Provided he controls these things in a way which does no long-term damage to the environment for himself or for other creatures then he should not be debarred, should not be kept out just because before the days of motor cars he could not reach certain areas, which were the lonely and wonderful preserves of the lucky few.

Pollution in Ramsgate marina

I will fight any project which seems to me to be unnecessary for the continuing well-being of my fellow men, or which seems to be unnecessarily sited. Reservoirs for instance, inevitably cause disturbance to some, loss of homes and livelihood to others, but for the greater good are essential. Modern reservoirs, such as Rutland Water, are ornamental lakes with facilities for fishing and boating, carefully landscaped and not a bit like the awful, rectangular, banked-up and sterile waterpounds that previous generations built. Even where enormous disturbance is made by removing gravel, sand, or other essential materials, in time these areas have to be returned to some kind

144

of natural state, either as lakes, or for agricultural use, so I would not oppose the extraction of such materials on the grounds of immediate damage to scenery and ecology, but look for the long-term advantages.

Also it is my experience that in spite of the outcry of some conservationists it is surprising how birds and even animals adapt themselves to changing surroundings, and how little disturbed most creatures turn out to be. One has only to watch the hovercraft crossing the sea or the mudflats at Pegwell Bay to see how little notice the local seabirds and waders take of it. In fact they wait for the hovercraft to cross the mud and then rush in to pick up the edible bits and pieces which it has stirred up to the surface. There are many such examples one could quote.

The policy of the National Trust in its Operation Neptune of buying up large areas of coastline so that they can control development thereon, is of course absolutely excellent, and provides the ideal balance between conservation and allowing access.

The education of the user to respect and take care of the world he lives in is the key to conservation and the prevention of pollution. On the small local scale this is not too difficult, and while there will always be litterbugs and despoilers, vandals and thieves, they are the minority, and I believe that the majority do prevail, even if it means going out and tidying up the mess themselves. What is far more difficult is the prevention of large-scale pollution, usually as a part of operations run for profit, as in the transport of crude oil across the oceans of the world and the ruthless and callous pollution which is a part of this. Pollution of rivers, coastlines and sea, which is what concerns me here, comes in so many ways.

A world which is perfectly aware of what major oil spills from supertankers, and the continuous minor spills, are doing to the sea and the coastlines is unable to stop it happening, but a country should be perfectly capable of preventing its towns and cities from emptying untreated or half-treated sewage into rivers and inshore waters and to stop factories large and small from putting filth, chemical and otherwise, into our rivers. It seems to be a matter of logical priorities. The transformation of London and other cities by the creation of smokeless zones is dramatic to anyone old enough to remember the post-war smogs and the pre-war fogs. That was a priority. But I cannot understand the logic which spends more than half a million pounds building up a shingle bank to protect a golf course, and makes no attempt to modernise the antique plant which pumps the chopped-up

145

Rubbish dumped on the saltmarsh channels at the mouth of the Kentish Stour

sewage of a town of 25,000 people through one pipe in that shingle bank to a point a couple of hundred yards offshore where it can swill up and down the coast with every tide. Or the logic which allows factories to be built a mile from the mouth of a river which empties into a partially enclosed bay, where once again the tidal streams can only spread the riverborne factory wastes up and down the beaches of several seaside resorts. Or the logic which allows the town waste of 50,000 people to be dumped on saltmarshes where high tides can get at it and add it to the sewage and factory waste already washing up and down the beach. None of these pollutions are unavoidable, and are therefore to be fought endlessly until they are reduced and finally eliminated. They exist all round our coasts. There are paradoxes; enormous efforts are being made to clean up the Thames and this difficult river is being steadily improved. Even the salmon are prospecting it. Yet down in the Thames estuary the Medway is badly polluted by its surrounding towns and empties its filth into the sea where it can wash back up into the Thames!

Most of our population knows little and cares less about pollution.

Those who live by sea and river cannot help but be aware of it. How many of us do anything about it is another matter. In relation to the size of the problem and the vested interests or apathy of those causing it, one feels puny. But voices raised in protest combine to make an irritating howl. Between major catastrophies, the dedicated keep the various societies and long-term protests going and act as watchdogs even if they can do nothing more effective than bark. Each 'incident' of serious pollution stirs more people to concern. In Britain there is much awareness in some government departments which try quite hard, but they are up against commercial interests national and international.

The waters upon the face of the earth are not a kind of disinfecting blanket, endlessly capable of regeneration and self cleansing as the complacent would have us believe. We have already succeeded in polluting all of them seriously. The remaining whales are still being hunted ruthlessly in spite of major efforts at conservation, but their final extinction will be by pollution when we poison their element beyond the tolerance of their mammalian bodies. If the ecologies of the sea, especially in the comparatively shallow waters around the continents and inshore, break down, then life as we know it on this planet is doomed. That is the most pessimistic view possible, but it all begins on shore; *we* do it. There will be no living by tidal waters when the seas are a lethal soup; when the estuaries are just stinking barren black mudflats, and the rocky shores and sandy bays are deserts of oil-encrusted waste.

FURTHER READING   Beedell, S. M. *Pick Cook and Brew* (Pelham); Hargreaves, B. (ed) *The Sporting Wife* (Witherby); McCaul and Crossland. *Water Pollution* (Harcourt Brace Jovanovich Inc); Lockley, R. M. *Whales, Dolphins & Porpoises* (David & Charles).

EQUIPMENT   *R. & B. Leakey,* Belle Hill, Settle, Yorks BD24 0BB (All types of pots and nets; home smokers).

USEFUL ADDRESSES   *The National Trust,* 42 Queen Anne's Gate, London SW1; *National Trust of Scotland,* 5 Charlotte Square, Edinburgh EH2 4DU; *Nature Conservancy Council,* 19 Belgrave Square, London SW1; *County Naturalists Trust* for each County, address in local library; *Seed the Sea Society,* Sec R. D. Leakey, Sutcliffe House, Settle, Yorks BD24 0BA.

8

Clothes

The traditional clothes of the longshoreman were, like his boats, developed for use, not show, and are now worn by many for show, not use. Nevertheless they are excellent and new materials have improved many of the garments (see illustration on page 140).

Starting at the skin, few men wear 'long johns' these days, although many women wear tights, and either do help to keep you warm in very cold weather, worn under trousers. A string vest allows a layer of air, heated up by your own body, to build up next to the skin, or there are wool or special mixture vests with long sleeves from firms which specialise in cold-weather underwear. Pure synthetics next to the skin act as a good insulating under layer until you sweat. The very windproofs which keep biting north-easterlies out, keep body moisture in, so that non-absorbent synthetic underwear soon becomes damp and cold. Wool or thick cotton or a mixture absorbs this moisture and breathes it out. Longshoremen's top wear is heavy serge trousers and a close-knitted guernsey, seaman's jumper or a heavy hand-knitted jumper of natural oiled wool. Over this most wear a slop shirt which is a square heavy-cotton loose-fitting garment, partially windproof, worn to protect the valuable guernsey from dirt and damage. Thick woolly socks knitted from oiled wool, under fairly loose-fitting wellington or thigh boots keep the feet warm. Thigh boots are worn turned down, and only tied up with a cord through an eyelet in the top when the wearer is wading or working in wet conditions. These boots themselves form a wind and waterproof layer and provided that they are not tight enough to cause constriction of clothes and body inside them, are very warm.

Nowadays rubber boots of light yet tough construction can be bought in all leg lengths and depending on use, the short leg length halfway up the calf is very useful.

Old-fashioned heavy and stiff oilskins have been completely replaced by synthetics and to keep out wind and wet there are various types of anoraks, parkas and overtrousers, and complete overall garments available. The latest are made of a synthetic material bonded to a stretchy back, which is light and flexible and actually 'breathes', allowing some body moisture to escape. In wet weather either your top garment must be long enough so that water from it does not drip down on to your trousers or into boots, or your trousers must also be waterproof and worn outside your boots. In emergency, dustbin liners tied on with string make passable overtrousers!

Breeches, fastened just below the knee, worn over tights and with long thick socks are warmer and more comfortable for walking and working than trousers. Wear a cotton shirt, and a light jumper, and then a heavy jumper as described. Be sure your jumpers are long enough and tight fitting round the lower body so they don't ride up and let in cold air. Guernseys and seamen's sweaters are deliberately made this way.

If it is not wet, only windy, then thin nylon windproofs over the top should keep you warm and are not too bulky. A pair of golf or cycling overtrousers tucked into boots, make a tremendous difference. In really cold weather or if you are to be stationary, fishing or bird watching or wildfowling perhaps, then the latest quilted duvet jackets are marvellous. The duvet waistcoat which leaves the arms free can be worn under a light windproof or a parka.

Headwear is very important as much body heat is lost through the head. Woolly hats or helmets worn under the light nylon hood of an anorak are adequate for cold weather. A helmet is especially good as it protects the back of the neck, and the chest. Nothing beats a souwester in the wet. Peaked hats *must* be waterproof and not liable to go soggy.

Gloves are essential in winter. If you need to be able to use your fingers to work a camera, bait hooks or whatever, then a pair of old gloves with the fingers cut off for an inch and a half to make mittens, are marvellous, as are specially knitted mittens. Wear them under loose sheepskin or leather mittens or gauntlets and you'll never get cold hands. Be sure not to lose the big gloves when you take them off to work. Slip them into a pocket or tuck them in the front of your anorak. Or best of all, have a ring or a tape on each top glove to which to tie each end of a cord which goes up one sleeve of your jacket, across your back and down the other.

Back to footwear: for walking, good lace-up leather boots are much better than wellingtons, provided they are kept thoroughly water-

A fully laden wildfowler well protected from the elements (*John Marchington*)

proof with dubbin or modern silicone spray. The latter is effective, but does not feed the leather. However good the waterproofing, salt does get into boots and leaves a kind of tidemark as they dry out. This makes them less water resistant because the salt in leather will always soak up water. And it eventually rots the stitching. So always scrub off seashore mud and sand when you take off your boots. To remove bad salt marks, rub the boots with a cut lemon, squeezing on plenty of juice, then wipe them dry, and leave to dry out completely in a warm, ventilated place, *not* on top of a radiator or stove. If they are wet inside

150

stuff them with crumpled newspaper, or with silica bags if available. Chemists sell silica which you can make up into small bags. Silica crystals are used between panes in double glazed windows to soak up condensation so if you have difficulty in getting them, try your nearest glazier – he might know where there is a supplier.

Showerproofing is just that. Showerproof clothes do not resist anything but light drizzle or mist, and the proofing goes when they are washed or cleaned. A good spray with a showerproofing aerosol restores some water resistance to close-woven fabrics, but is useless on loosely woven materials.

Summer wear is a matter of personal preference. Canvas shoes rot quickly if constantly wet with sea water, and washing in fresh water does help to prolong their life a little. Our weather changes so quickly, so, on the water or far from home, always take just one more sweater (or even a light anorak) than you think you could possibly need. In hot sunshine you will sunburn faster on the water than on shore because the sea reflects the sun's rays back at you. Never go out sailing or fishing without taking a long-sleeved shirt and put it on the moment you begin to burn. There is rarely any shade in a small boat, and a light wide-brimmed hat helps to prevent a badly sunburned face. Lips are specially vulnerable and anti-sunburn cream should always be carried and used. Lipsalve or Nivea helps to ease the discomfort of already sunburned lips. Another vulnerable area is the thighs. When you are sitting in a boat in shorts or bathing costume, the sun really seems to catch them, so do use plenty of anti-sunburn cream or oil on all exposed parts of the body.

For winter wear I include two unusual but excellent knitting patterns from 'Helping the Trawlers' from the Royal National Mission to Deep Sea Fishermen, published eighty years ago.

THE UHLAN CAP

> 'This Uhlan Cap – nor Uhlan Cap alone,
> But helmet, comforter and cap in one.'

The accompanying illustrations will make clearer than any more verbal description, the force and appropriateness of the couplet, and the annexed working details will enable our readers to utilise their skill in the preparation of this most useful article for the winter.

Use pure wool, double knitting or other fairly thick soft wool and 4 needles pointed at both ends, No 8s or 9s, according to size required.

151

" This Uhlan Cap—nor Uhlan Cap alone,
But helmet, comforter, and cap in one."

The Uhlan cap: old-fashioned but still practical

Cast on 30 stitches – 10 on each of 3 needles.
Rounds 1 and 2. Knit 4, purl 1, repeat to end of round
Round 3. Make 1, knit 4, make 1, purl 1, repeat to end of round
Rounds 4, 5, 6. Knit 6, purl 1, repeat to end of round
Round 7. Make 1, knit 6, make 1, purl 1, repeat
Rounds 8, 9, 10. Knit 8, purl 1, repeat
Round 11. Make 1, knit 8, purl 1, repeat
Rounds 12, 13, 14. Knit 10, purl 1, repeat
Round 15. Make 1, knit 10, make 1, purl 1, repeat
Rounds 16, 17, 18. Knit 12, purl 1, repeat
Round 19. Make 1, knit 12, make 1, purl 1, repeat
Round 20. Make 1, knit 14, purl 1, repeat
   There should now be 96 stitches on the needles.
Knit 2, purl 2, every round till the work measures exactly 6in from the
beginning of the cap.
Cast off 30 stitches loosely to make the opening for the face; knit 2,

152

purl 2, backwards and forwards for 8 rows (about 1in). Cast on 30 stitches loosely, and knit 2, purl 2, every round till the total length is 21in. Cast off loosely. Pass a piece of wool through all the stitches of the opening at the top of the cap, draw up tightly, and sew together.

MITTENS

These mittens are greatly valued by the men. The oilskins they are compelled to wear, by reason of the incessant wetting with sea water grow hard and cruel; the wrist, frayed by the oilskin, is scarified, and the salt water reaching the wound produces 'sea blister' an excessively painful sore. When however woollen mittens are worn, the 'sea blister' is seldom known and much suffering is consequently avoided.

The mittens are made as follows:

Use pure double knitting wool or oiled wool and 4 needles, No 12s. Greys, drabs and heather mixtures are preferable to wools with bright dyes.

Cast 52 stitches on 3 needles, and knit 2 plain and 2 purl for 36 rounds. This forms the wrist.
Knit 15 plain rounds; then knit the thumb thus:
Round 1. Knit 2, make 1, knit 2, make 1, then knit to end
Rounds 2 and 3. Plain
Round 4. Knit 2, make 1, knit 4, make 1, then knit to end
Rounds 5 and 6. Plain
Round 7. Knit 2, make 1, knit 6, make 1, then to end
Rounds 8 and 9. Plain
Round 10. Knit 2, make 1, knit 8, make 1, then knit to end
Rounds 11 and 12. Plain
Round 13. Knit 2, make 1, knit 10, make 1, then knit to end
Rounds 14 and 15. Plain
Round 16. Knit 2, make 1, knit 12, make 1, then knit to end
Rounds 17 and 18. Plain
Round 19. Knit 2, make 1, knit 14, make 1, then knit to end
Rounds 20 and 21. Plain
Round 22. Knit 2, make 1, knit 16, make 1, then knit to end
Rounds 23 and 24. Plain
Round 25. Knit 2, make 1, knit 18, make 1, then knit to end
Rounds 26 and 27. Plain
Round 28. Knit 2, make 1, knit 20, make 1, then knit to end
Rounds 29 and 30. Plain
Round 31. Knit 2, make 1, knit 22, make 1, then knit to end

Round 32. Knit 3, then slip off on a bit of wool, 22 stitches, and knit plain the rest of the round
Then knit 10 rounds plain.
Then knit 10 rounds, 2 plain and 2 purl, and cast off loosely.
Then knit the rest of the thumb thus: take up the 22 stitches off the wool on to 3 needles, adding 2 more stitches where the opening is, which will make 8 stitches on each needle. Knit 6 rounds plain.
Then knit 6 rounds, 2 plain and 2 purl, and cast off loosely.

Fasten off the ends.

9

Safety, Swimming and Rescue

Floods

Anyone who has ever been in a flood knows that water out of control, out of its proper places, is utterly terrifying. The North Sea surge of 12 January 1978 caused serious flooding where I live. It happened in the middle of the night which made it all the worse, and it was not just a case of an exceptionally rough sea on a spring tide throwing a few great waves over the sea-front and sand dunes. The whole sea rose higher than it should and the shoreline was overwhelmed. Great thundering waves raced inland carrying away everything in their path, from solid brick walls and miles of shingle, to boats beached way above the tideline. A friend whose house had been swept through by the flood said, 'It's bad enough being in a ship in a rough sea, but have you ever tried being in a *house* in a rough sea?'

Water coming the other way, caused by unusually heavy or prolonged rainfall, as happens frequently in this country, causes at least three or four severe river floods every winter. These are also destructive and frightening, especially in estuaries when the tide comes in and holds back the land water. It is always such combinations of circumstances which cause the worst flooding: spring tides, high winds blowing onshore, heavy rainfall on land where the water table is already high after prolonged rain, and sudden changes in atmospheric pressure. Therefore to some extent they are possible to foretell, at least a few hours ahead. The exact magnitude of the flood is not possible to judge beforehand. The Meteorological Office, river boards and local authorities do try to issue flood warnings on a regional scale and locally. In some vulnerable areas arrangements have been made for loudspeaker vans with klaxons to race round waking people up or warning of imminent flooding, and householders have been issued with sandbags. However, if you live anywhere which is the faintest bit likely to be flooded, take your own precautions.

Your house may seem to be well above high water mark, but do check to see if the water has ever reached your level, however many years ago. What has happened once may happen again. Look for tell-tale high tide marks on both inside and outside walls. If outside walls have been painted any distance up from the bottom with tar or bitumen paint (which is water resistant) it could be a sign of occasional flooding.

If you live at the foot of a hill or even part way down it, make sure that there could be no possibility of flooding from above in very heavy rain. It was this type of flooding which swept Lynmouth into the sea. Make sure that water can flow away without impediment. A garden wall or hedge across the fall of the ground might make a dam which would eventually give way and release a flood. Far better for there to be open ground down which water can run clean away. A few sandbags around doors which face uphill is then enough to help keep water out of the house.

Sandbags are a good protection against flood water. If your home is liable to flood then it is worth having metal flood-doors made which can be dropped into angle-iron channelling in front of the door and held in place with a couple of bolts. Such precautions may not be needed very often, but can save an awful lot of mess and trouble. Once is enough.

If you are caught in a sudden flood, you may have to make for higher ground, or abandon your car, or even climb a tree. Flash floods which come suddenly as a wall of racing water happen where flood water has been dammed up and has then broken through. Depending on where you are of course, it may be that the first terrifying rush of water will subside to a steady flow, in which case stay in your car till you can safely move to higher ground. If the flood water continues to rise slowly, then get back away from it to higher ground, never try to go on through it either in a car or on foot.

At home it is best to stay indoors, moving everything movable upstairs if you have time, and making no attempt to swim or wade for it if the water is running fast or still rising. The time to try for escape is when the flood is on the wane, even then look out for potholes scoured out by the water, and in any case by then there will be boats, emergency services, etc, to help you. Local radio, if you have it in your area, may be issuing warnings and advice, so keep it on.

If your house is flooded, turn off the electricity at the main. Water and electricity do not go together and much damage can be done, even

The power of the sea: brick wall in ruins after a gale

fires started. Turn off gas supplies at the main, because pilot lights may be flooded and go out, and then remain unlit when the flood subsides.

If you have to take to the top storey, make sure you take up drinking water, food, a portable stove, warm and waterproof clothing, and torches or lamps. If you have time, fill every Thermos flask available with tea, coffee, soup, hot milk, etc.

Check your insurance policies to be certain that you are fully covered against damage by flood. It is not always the case. Remember that quite apart from structural damage to floors, walls, windows, etc, and ruined carpets and furniture, everything electrical may have to be junked from the vacuum cleaner to the deep-freezer (and its contents). Motor cars are particularly vulnerable, especially to sea water. Nothing will remain undamaged except for hardware and ceramics, everything else can suffer damage according to how long it is immersed. Even plain wooden furniture won't take more than a gentle soaking, and anyway the water will more than likely be full of mud, muck and even sewage.

It is the aftermath which is so depressing. Sodden carpets, filthy furniture and ruined books. Take out everything and hang it where it can dry, and wash everything washable. Do not wash electric motors. Petrol engines may be washed, in fact should be, if sea water has got at them. Electric motors cannot be successfully dried out unless the water damage is merely a few splashes. Several hours in front of a fan heater might just do the trick.

Walls and floors that have been soaked must be allowed to dry completely, and they will never quite do this if sea water has got into them. Always take up some floorboards in a flooded floor to allow the cavity beneath to dry out. It may appear that the floor is not too bad, but in a week or so the mud, water, etc, which has got underneath will begin to stink and sweat, as well as the boards themselves. If this happens then they must be replaced. Mud and pollution from drains can be washed away and eventually cleaned up, but salt persists and because it is hygroscopic it absorbs atmospheric moisture in humid weather, carrying it into brickwork, etc, thus causing stains on wallpaper and blooms of salt on almost any kind of surface (see page 219).

If you keep boats or gear above high water mark, normally perfectly safe, then take some flood precautions. At times of extra high tide or storm, when there is a warning, there are usually plenty of people to help move their own and each other's boats out of reach of the water. It is the sudden flood that does the damage, so if there is even the very faintest possibility of this, then leave your boat moored, anchored, or tied fore and aft, on ropes long enough to allow the boat to rise in flood water, but not to crash into other boats or solid obstructions. If your boat is normally moored or tied up against a jetty or left on mud at low water, then be sure that the mooring lines are long enough to allow her to rise to any flood without being pulled under. Of course it is not possible to guard against every eventuality, but there is a lot that you can do. Loose gear of any kind left lying around will probably be lost or damaged in a flood, and may cause damage to other property.

Swimming and Water Safety

Of course the best place to learn to swim is in a swimming pool. No danger of being swept off one's feet or swamped by waves, and the comforting presence of the pool's side and the instructor, possibly using a safety harness in the early stages, gives the beginner the one thing which is necessary before he can learn to swim – confidence. That applies at any age. The smallest baby, provided mother is there and he is supported in a floatation garment of some kind, is perfectly confident in the water, and it is only later on that confidence can be destroyed. Toddlers, taken to the sea's edge, find the waves huge, terrifying and cold, and to carry a small child struggling into the enormous sea is probably the best way to destroy his confidence for years. Adults who cannot swim well are all the more aware of the very real dangers of drowning, and equally lack confidence. So, if possible, at any age, learn to swim in a pool. For if you are to live by tidal waters, then not only for their own safety, but for their endless pleasure, the whole family should be able to swim.

We live in liquid before we are born, and according to the scientists, if not the book of Genesis, life on this planet came up out of the seas. Most animals swim naturally, but man, strangely, does not. Yet it is the easiest thing in the world to float on water and to move around in it, provided you relax, and breathe normally, and make natural paddling movements with hands and feet. For many there is great pleasure in swimming, not only the extended and enlarged pleasures of skin diving and sub aqua swimming or surfing, but that of just being in the water. For heavyweights, the density of water makes them weightless. It supports the limbs and the whole body so that the strain is taken from muscles and bones, and aches and pains disappear. Any rheumatic sufferer who has swum in hot thermal water knows how wonderful it is.

Salutary notice at Wells–next–the–Sea

Yet all this is a far cry from swimming in our cold sea except in the height of summer, and from swimming in muddy estuary water.

The best possible place, failing a swimming pool, to start small children swimming, is in a nice warm rock pool a couple of feet deep. Let them paddle and splash, and encourage them to float on their backs and fronts, with hands on the bottom. Provide blow–up arm floats or even small lifejackets, making sure that any lifejacket cannot have the effect of turning the child head down in the water. In other words it must fit properly and be tied on so that it cannot slip off the shoulders and down the body. Lifejackets which are too big can be lethal. A large chunk of expanded polystyrene foam makes an excellent float for a child to hold while he paddles along with his feet. Anything does which gives a child the necessary feeling of confidence in the water, and assurance that he can actually stay on the surface without touching the bottom. After a while, but without pressing the point, reduce the support until the child is splashing and swimming about without any articifial help. The one way *not* to teach a child to swim, is to demonstrate a kind of breast stroke to him, hold him under the chin and expect him to struggle along in what is a totally unnatural position. The child must become used to lifting his head only slightly, enough to breathe, and occasionally submerging. It is not a bad exercise to stand waist deep in water and dip the head under, with the eyes open, blow a load of bubbles, lift the head, breathe and repeat the process till being under water is fun. A pair of swimming goggles helps here because the moment the head is submerged the exciting underwater world, even of a sandy pool, is instantly revealed.

Steady and rhythmic breathing and body relaxation are the secrets of swimming, and an adult learning to swim finds it easier to practise and control breathing than does a child, but harder to achieve the necessary body relaxation. The moment the muscles tense in the water, and this can happen to the best of swimmers in moments of panic, then the body seems to loose buoyancy and sink. I know someone who is not at all a strong swimmer, and is a little scared of the water, yet finds that she swims far better and is more relaxed when she wears snorkel and flippers. This is because the whole body, and head, floating slightly arched on the water, with lungs filling and emptying rhythmically, moved gently along by a natural paddling motion of the flippered feet, themselves made buoyant by the flippers, is totally relaxed and natural. The moment she lifts up her head and tries to swim in the choppy surface water, she becomes tense and can only swim a few strokes.

Perhaps the biggest advantage of learning to swim in the sea is that salt water is denser than fresh water, so the body is more buoyant and it is easier to stay on the surface.

Unless they have been taught in a swimming pool when very young, few children become even remotely competent sea swimmers before they are eight or nine years old. Those who are taught to waterski young and wear wet suits, usually swim early, partly because a wet suit provides a certain amount of buoyancy and makes swimming easy.

Flippers are a wonderful aid at all ages, and I would recommend that all those who swim in the sea should learn to use them at all times, even in heavy surf. They give the swimmer so much extra power, and are only clumsy when one is entering or leaving the water, or trying to walk along in the shallows. My elder daughter, who had lived near the sea and became used to the water from the time she could walk, could never swim more than a few strokes until she was ten. The North Devon sea was always rough and frightening, and the rock pools not

161

big enough. Then one day I bought her some flippers and she tried them in a sea-water-filled swimming pool at Bude, and she went straight across it without stopping. From then on her swimming became more and more confident and powerful. My younger daughter lives by a sea which in summer is usually calm right inshore, and could swim and use flippers from the age of eight.

Children who are likely to spend time in boats, especially sailing dinghies, must be able to swim, and must also be able to swim in lifejackets. This is not particularly easy, because a lifejacket lifts the body high out of the water, and tends to float the body in a fairly upright position. It becomes impossible to do any proper swimming stroke, which normally requires the head to be submerged part of the time. The best that can be done is either a kind of short breast stroke, or an overarm flail, with plenty of kicking from feet and legs. It is for this very reason that, although one always stays afloat in a lifejacket, swimming effectively against the tide or current for any distance is very difficult indeed, so the rule is *always,* when capsized, *stay with the boat.*

Many schools teach swimming, and while this is of course a very good thing, take care with the child who has become competent swimming in a pool, and perhaps has a couple of badges to prove it, the first few times he swims in the sea. Sea conditions are so very different and if there are any tides or currents, or any amount of surf, can be dangerous. A child who finds he cannot make headway against a current, is likely to panic and soon become exhausted and in serious trouble. So do take care to point out any likely difficulties and dangers, and explain that notice boards which discourage swimming at certain states of the tide and red danger flags hoisted when the sea is too rough, are not put there just for fun however innocuous the sea may look. Even strong swimmers should take careful heed of such signs unless they know exactly what they are doing and what the dangers are. Never try to beat a current, never swim against it; you will soon become too tired to continue swimming and will lose any ground you have gained in just a few moments. Swim diagonally across a current towards safety, or go with it if possible till it carries you to another part of the beach. Close inshore, where small freshwater streams run across sand or mud into the sea, a rip very often forms when the tide covers the beach. Effectively, because the bottom is a little deeper there, the water which has come up the beach in waves runs back just a little faster down that channel, and creates a current sweeping fast out to sea, not usually very wide or very long, but enough to take a swimmer into deep water. Always swim sideways when caught in a rip. Don't try to get back inshore, just swim out of it into currentless water, and then swim in.

On a steep beach the undertow caused by the water rushing back down and beneath the incoming waves can cause problems, dragging the unwary out and down in a most unpleasant way. There can be an undertow at dead low water on an apparently level beach, where it suddenly slopes away to deeper water. Estuaries may look safe enough at high tide and when the tide is coming in, as the water will be moving upstream into the rivers, and if it takes you up, it should be possible to swim sideways to the bank. It is on the ebb tide when the sea water returns to its proper place, pushed at extra speed by the dammed-up river water, that it becomes dangerous and can soon sweep the unwary out to sea. In any case, river-mouth swimming is not to be recommended for there are usually dangerous banks and bars. Where the

Young wildfowlers negotiating mud with proper care (*John Marchington*)

estuary is muddy then no one wants to swim anyway, and the mud itself may be very dangerous and deep enough to trap the unwary. Quicksands are not always marked and can suddenly be there as the tide comes in, and the water moves into the sand turning it into a kind of bottomless sludge. At first you can avoid sinking if you run across the surface, but never venture on to known quicksands when the tide is about to flow.

In estuaries and saltmarshes there are usually quite deep creeks which fill at high tide, but at low water contain only a dribble at the bottom and deep, grey mud at the sides. It is dangerous indeed to try to cross such creeks unless you know exactly how deep the mud is. If caught in mud and unable to get your feet out, spread your body across the mud as much as possible and try to 'swim out'. It is a dangerous situation and one which you should not get into. Children who are allowed to play along muddy creeks should be made well aware of the danger; although they are lighter and do not sink so readily, they can still become trapped.

To rescue anyone trapped in mud or quicksand, don't get caught yourself, that is no help. Try to get a rope to the person, having first tied a loop in it that can be slipped over the head and under the armpits. Boards, ladders, any old bits of timber should be pushed out towards the victim to make a support for rescuers to get near. Your own coat and clothing, any old sacks, bits of polythene sheet, even matted

All kinds of craft are at home in Brightlingsea harbour

lumps of seaweed should be thrown to the victim to make some kind of carpet of support on to which he can get his arms and upper body to prevent further sinking. Never forget, if there is a helicopter rescue service available anywhere in your area, that a helicopter is fast and effective for getting someone out of mud or quicksand if they can get there in time, and also for lifting people from apparently inaccessible places on cliff sides.

All kinds of airbeds, tyres, small inflatable boats, are dangerous when used if the wind is offshore, or where there are currents. A child can be carried from shallow water into deep water or surf in a moment, and may then be swept off or just fall off in a panic. A large rubber ball being played with in the edge of the sea may be blown just out of reach and a weak swimmer is soon out of his depth trying to get it. Once a ball starts to blow across the surface in the wind it is obviously going to move much faster than any swimmer, so it is a hopeless pursuit in any case. Let it go, it is not worth a life.

It surely goes without saying that any child who is going off to play with canoes, boats, rafts, or even along the water's edge if it is deep, should always wear a lifejacket. The habit of wearing a jacket, like wearing a safety belt in a car, may take some forming and there are still far too many people who go fishing and power boating without wearing their jackets. Some don't even bother to carry them in the boat. There is no more potentially dangerous set-up than a small, light GRP dinghy, with far too many people in it, all without lifejackets, bobbing about on the end of too short an anchor cable in an offshore rising wind, fishing as the tide comes in. Yet around our coasts one sees it all the time. Another all too common sight is the overloaded small 'toy' inflatable dinghy, probably with four or five children and two small paddles which they cannot use, going away fast downtide, with the children frantically paddling against it.

To sum up: learn to swim, in clothing as well as a bathing costume, wear a lifejacket in a small boat, take note of warning notices and flags. When swimming don't over-reach yourself, don't try to swim too far or in too rough a sea. Stay with your boat.

Cliff Dangers

Although this book is more concerned with estuaries and beaches than with cliffs, there are frequent accidents and strandings on our cliffs and much tragedy and trouble therefrom. Cliffs may look quite easy to climb from below, usually because cliff falls have made jumbled ledges of rock or chalk, or slopes of sand. The unwary, usually a youngster who decides to go up, all too often find that he reaches a point where the cliff becomes sheer and unclimbable; or realises on looking down that he has a long way to fall and becomes paralysed with vertigo or terror. The rule is never to climb cliffs of any type, however low, where there is no distinct proper path, and to instill in the young that they are very dangerous places. Sometimes an attempt is made to get down from the top, and this is even more dangerous as it is just never possible to see all the way down the face of a cliff, however sloping, from the top. Chalk cliffs may crumble suddenly and sand cliffs dissolve under the feet. Both types often have dangerous overhangs tufted with grass roots because the soil at the top is held together by matted grass and the subsoil of sand or chalk beneath has fallen away. Never go near the edge of a cliff. There is no point in it and it is potentially lethal. Take care of small children anywhere within a hundred yards of a cliff's edge, and watch out for ball games, etc, which might take a child too near. All but the most sedate dogs should be kept on a lead. I have seen rabbits and even foxes disappear over the cliff's edge at Beachy Head to burrows which only they can reach. An excited dog chasing one in such a place just could not make it.

Never park your car directly facing or backing on to a cliff edge. It can so easily run straight down over if the brakes slip. In fact just do not take cars anywhere near the edge of a cliff, and in places where apparently usable unmade roads go down diagonally, don't use them. They have probably been made by donkeys and carts or tractors going down for seaweed, or even for quarrying purposes just a few yards down the cliff, and once down there with a car you might not be able to turn or even reverse back. This applies particularly in the West Country.

It should go without saying, but happens so often, that one should not go for walks under cliffs when the tide is coming in or likely to come in before you return or get to the next way out. Too many people have to be rescued from precarious perches along tide-washed cliffs. If you are caught and cannot attract attention, then just get somewhere above high tide mark (look at the rocks for sign of land plants) and wait for the tide to go out again. Children should be warned against this because they are too inexperienced to stop to consider such things.

(Opposite) Spritsail barge in the Thames estuary

Soft Sand

I carry a tow rope in my car, so can help either to rescue stranded cars or provide the means for my own rescue if I am foolish enough to get stranded, which has happened several times.

Unless your car is a Land Rover or something of the kind with four-wheel drive, it is asking for trouble to take it on to sand or shingle. Cars with big radial tyres are less likely to get stuck in sand than cars with ordinary road tyres, and the so-called beach buggies have special tyres suitable for sand and shingle.

Even a small patch of sand in what appears to be grass can catch you, and once the car wheels begin to spin, the grass turns out to be just a thin layer and your car is stuck. All the revving in the world merely digs a deeper grave for the back wheels, and once the underside of the car touches the ground, it is even harder to extricate it. You can help yourself a bit. The moment the wheels begin to spin, stop. Get out and have a look at things. If it appears at all possible, try to reverse out, even a foot or two gained could be a help. Before rushing forward again put anything you can find in front of the wheels – stones, pieces of wood, cloth, hay, straw, old string nets, or even the floor mats from your car – and make sure the ruts are dug away at the front to a slope and not a cliff. Get all your passengers to push, and try to drive out in second gear; don't rev up more than is necessary to prevent the engine stalling, it just digs worse holes. If you are irretrievably stuck, then find a bit of wood or a big stone to support the base of your jack, and jack the car up until one wheel is well clear of the rut. Fill the rut with whatever solid rubbish you can find, lower the jack, and repeat the process on the other wheels, thus bringing them up to surface level again. Then, laying a track of hard rubbish in front of the wheels, if possible, just drive away.

If none of this works, you will just have to abandon ship and go for help. To tow a car out of trouble, attach the tow rope to a towing eye or a towbar on your own car if you have one, and then to the car to be towed by passing it around both bumper brackets. If it is just tied to the bumper it will probably wrench it off or bend it. Make sure the towing car is on firm ground, and then move slowly forward in bottom gear, taking up the strain gently. Signal for the driver of the stuck car to rev up gently and slip his car in gear and for all helpers to push. It usually takes only a little 'tweak' to get a sand-bogged car out of trouble. If your own wheels start to spin and your clutch to slip, then do a little more digging to smooth the path of the stranded car.

If a car has been stuck in sea sand or mud, or has been even slightly flooded, then give it the most thorough hosing with fresh water as soon as possible. Sea water causes dreadful rust, and if it has got into the electrics of a car they will almost certainly have to be replaced.

If you have driven your car on sand, be sure that it has not got into brakes or into universal joints in the back axle. If it has it will eventually cause wear and disintegration. Wet sea-water mud can also cause damage by carrying salt into metal parts, although it is finer than sand and will not cause so much abrasive damage to moving parts.

Shingle may look perfectly solid at the top of a beach but no normal car will travel on it for more than a few feet without becoming stuck.

Warn helpers who are pushing your car to look out for bits of rubbish or stones chucked out by the wheels as they spin, and also not to fall flat on their faces if the car does suddenly move off.

Rescue at Sea

It is important to know how to approach and pick up someone who is in the water. If possible always go uptide towards them, keeping way on on your boat, either with sails, oars or motor so that the person in the water is drifting down towards you and not floating away. If in a sailing boat, with the wind coming with the tide, then beat up towards the swimmer and luff alongside at the last moment. This calls for good judgement. Otherwise sail towards him and at the last moment slacken right off or luff up so that your boat comes gently to him and he drifts along your uptide side. In a powered boat, with head to tide, it is easier and safer to meet someone drifting down towards you so that he floats down your uptide side and can be taken in over it, rather than over the stern where there is danger from the propeller.

It is exactly the same drill, really, as coming to a mooring, or picking up a buoy on a crab pot, or even up to a bank or jetty. Never let yourself be swept towards it by the tide, but always come up slowly under wind or engine power and lose way at the last moment. Practise this manoeuvre from all directions to an anchored buoy, and then try dropping a buoy overboard unanchored, and let it drift away from you for a hundred yards before initiating recovery. Go after the buoy and past it before rounding uptide to recover it.

In any sailing boat larger than a dinghy, if you lose a man overboard, throw out a lifebelt, and then gybe. No matter what your point of sailing, gybe, so that as you round up towards the person in the water, almost all way is off the boat, and it is easy to gentle the boat back to

169

recover the one in the water. Only in an unstable dinghy is it not a good idea to gybe, because a gybe, especially when done in heavy weather and perhaps off a reach or even a beat, and in a bit of a hurry, can easily result in a capsize, with two or three people in the water instead of one.

It is not the easiest thing in the world to haul someone back into a small boat. Unless the boat is very stable it is best to bring the person in over the bow or the stern, making sure the propeller is not in gear. Or if there are several people in the boat, then move them to the opposite side to help balance it at the moment when the person leaves the water and all his weight pulls the side of the boat down. Racing dinghy sailors should have practised recovery drill and should know the best way to get back into their own boats. It does rather depend on type. Power boats usually carry boat ladders especially if used for waterskiing. If the one in the water is still full of strength, then just tie a big loop in any piece of rope, perhaps the painter or halfway along the anchor cable or mainsheet, and drop this over, so that he can put his foot in it. Take a turn inboard round a cleat or a samson post, and then as he gets his hands on the gunwale and you heave him by the scruff of the neck, he can use the loop as a step to gain purchase. Even if there are two people in the boat, this loop dropped over the side can be a great help and avoid a lot of bruising and scraping for the one in the water. If he is too tired to help himself, then someone from the boat may have to go in to help, but a big loop tied with a bowline which can be dropped right over the head and arms of the person in the water will help those in the boat to pull him in, or at any rate to prevent him from drifting away again.

Whatever the condition of the rescued person, once he is in your boat warmth is very important, so wrap him up in something, wet clothes and all. Of course if you have a survival blanket, use that. Give hot sweet drinks if available, but *not* alcohol. Rub hands and feet if they are cold, and get the person ashore as fast as possible.

If you recover an unconscious person, lay him flat and administer the kiss of life (and heart massage if you know how) till breathing and heartbeat are re-established. This is not the place to describe how these first aids are done. Nowadays some schools teach them, and there are details in all first aid and swimming manuals. All who live by the water should familiarise themselves with the techniques by which so many lives have been saved. A short course in first aid is never a bad thing.

Towing Other Boats

To tow a sailing dinghy back to base is easy enough, provided there is some point of attachment for a tow rope well forward in the boat. Failing a towing eye, dinghies usually have carrying handles, and a rope passed through one, round the base of the mast, and out through the other, and then tied back on itself forward of the stem, makes a towing bridle. This distributes the pull evenly and should not tear the handles out of the deck. If a dinghy is waterlogged, this can happen all too easily if the tow rope is attached to a cleat or to something not designed to take the strain.

Fishing boats almost always have samson posts built in, round which a couple of turns of tow rope may be made. Always pass the line forward through a fair-lead if possible as a tow from the side makes the towed boat yaw about and difficult to drag along, especially if it is half full of water. Never tow too fast. It is not particularly funny to race along in a power boat with a dinghy designed to do not more than about 10 knots flat out, yawing and smashing along behind you in a cloud of spray. Tow steadily and gently, and if in a light following sea, try to keep the tension taut as the towed boat surfs, otherwise it will

The Orwell estuary: barges old and ancient, yachts and houseboats

bear down on you with the line slack and be in danger of fouling your propeller. Unfortunately if you try to tow too fast in a big following sea, while you have better steerage way and control, there is always a danger of being 'pooped' if the seas are breaking. In other words the following seas break over the stern of your boat and the towed boat and swamp them. Quite honestly rather than trying to tow, in a big following sea it is better to head into it and ride it out, or tow into the sea to another landfall.

Big power boat engines do not run happily at slow speeds for very long, and little outboards rarely have enough power to move two boats through the water, especially into the wind or any strong tide or current. Only the inboard engine designed to run at slow speeds, has the reliability and power to cope with a prolonged or heavy tow safely. So, even with the best of intentions, do not undertake to tow if you think it will be too much for your boat. Far better to anchor and stand by the other boat and fire off the distress flares which you should be carrying, to summon more powerful help. Two helpless boats are less use than one helpless boat, and should weather conditions worsen while you are standing by, then the other boat's crew can be taken aboard, and the stricken craft left at anchor, or even drifting if it cannot be anchored. Better to save lives than property.

Apart from flares, there are recognised distress signals. The continuous waving of a lifejacket, or, at night, the flashing of a light in a continuous series of three short and three long flashes. Whistle or hooter blasts in the same sequence. Any item of clothing hauled up the mast is a recognised distress signal, and lifeboats have been launched before now to the aid of a fisherman drying his shirt, all unknowing. The flying of an ensign upside down is also a recognised distress signal, but one that a small boat is unlikely to use.

Should you, from on shore, spot anything unusual, flares, smoke signals, hooters, flashings, wavings of any kind, act. Don't stand there wondering what is going on or whether you should do anything. Take note of the position of the distress signal in relation to some object on shore, note the bearing even roughly if you know how, get to a phone and dial 999 and ask for coastguards or police. Tell them what you have seen and leave it to them to make decisions. They will probably ask you to stay where you are till they arrive, but of course if you are anywhere near a sailing club, or other boats with people around, go and tell them what you have seen. Someone may be able to launch a fast boat to go directly to the assistance of the boat in trouble.

Coastguards and lifeboatmen prefer that you call them immediately, even on a wild goose chase, than that you wait and wonder if you really ought while people drown. In sea rescues time is vital, and a couple of minutes might make all the difference.

If someone is in trouble in the water, just offshore, crying for help or waving an arm, then you may have to take direct action to reach them with a rescue line or a boat. Move quickly but always enlist the help of anyone and everyone about, making sure that someone gets to a phone and calls for help via 999. In cases of possible drowning demand an ambulance or medical help straight away.

All too familiar are small groups of people looking out to sea wondering if that fishing boat or dinghy is in trouble or not, and yet fearing to take action because it might turn out to be nothing and they would feel foolish.

Of course those who only race dinghies under the auspices of a club do not normally go afloat except when there is a rescue boat on the water, or immediately available. There is usually some safety-conscious club member keeping an eye on things, and two-way radio from rescue boat to shore is now the rule rather than the exception. If any members of your family are going out in a boat, fishing, sailing or just pottering, then ask for an approximate arrival home time. 'Will you be back for lunch, or are you staying out till teatime?' That sort of query won't cause arguments. If a boat is well overdue home, then go and see if it is in sight, and if it is not, alert the coastguards. Don't leave it for several hours and until after dark before you do something. It is easier to find a boat in daylight. Even if there is nothing wrong, and your party have just stayed out much longer than they said, they will be a bit shattered when the inshore rescue boat arrives to ask if they are all right and are much more likely to be punctual in future. By the same token, always tell someone roughly where you are going and when you expect to be back, even in fine calm weather and if you get caught out and perhaps have to run ashore somewhere other than your home port, then do go straight to a phone and get a message home that you are all right. It can save a lot of worry and trouble.

FURTHER READING Summers, D. *East Coast Floods* (David & Charles); Johnson, Dick. *Seasafety* (Stanford Maritime); Haylock, Capt E. F. *Water Wisdom* (Pelham).

10

Water Sports

Sub Aqua, Skin Diving and Aqualung Diving

The first time you put on a face mask and dip your head below the surface of the water is a superb moment of discovery as you enter another world. Even if you happen to be looking into an empty sea over a deserted bottom, the light in the water is something you have never seen before. It is a personal discovery and never ceases to be, which is what makes sub aqua or underwater swimming a booming sport wherever it is possible.

To begin with, all you need is a good face mask and snorkel of the mouth-breathing type, and a pair of swim fins. It takes little time to master the art of steady breathing with the face submerged, and the relaxed slightly arched body position in which you float along the top of the water, using gentle movements of the fins and twists of the body to progress and change direction. Next you learn to dive, holding your breath and equalising pressure by blowing into your pinched nose, ascending and blowing to clear the snorkel tube. Perhaps you may never go beyond this point for there is plenty to see even along the rock edges or over the sand the moment your head is down and you have joined Cousteau in the magic depths!

Being natural predators, many people must progress to the spear gun, and to hunting for crabs and lobsters and (in some places) clams, but to do this effectively or achieve the limited freedom of the element you are looking in on from its edges, then you must learn to use an aqualung.

To dive alone is extremely foolish and risky, so join a club. Aqualung equipment, wet suits, boats, etc, are expensive, but well worth the money. The British Sub Aqua Club has plenty of local branches where you can get instruction and take a graduated course of certified proficiency tests, and where the diving is under the control of

174

those who know what they are doing. Provided you have no ear or heart trouble and are healthy enough to pass a basic medical, age is immaterial, and there should be no problems. You must first know how to swim to a certain standard.

To master the full techniques of aqualung diving takes a little time, during which you will, with your club, sample the different things to be done underwater.

Firstly there is just the fascination of being there, and seeing the new world under the dark surface of the sea. For some that is enough. Most wish to progress, some to hunting, but others (although no one passes by a large and juicy lobster) to photography. Photography requires underwater cameras and ever more expensive and better equipment, lights, etc, but increases the interest and pleasure of diving a thousand-fold.

Probably linked with photography, but not necessarily, are a variety of natural history studies. Some, such as a recent study of kelp masterminded by the naturalist David Bellamy, are done on a national scale to help the scientists with their ecological studies of the sea, especially just offshore. These studies are absolutely vital as the effects of man and his various effluents, intentional or accidental, on the ecology of the sea may be all too soon affecting his chances of comfortable survival on this planet.

Marine archaeology takes several forms, from the discovery, study and excavations of old wrecks to that of sunken villages. Others hunt for more recent wrecks, hopefully seeking salvage or treasure. Wrecks usually abound in marine life, so all sub aqua clubs like them.

Unfortunately the law is not very detailed or protective in regard to divers, except where they own the wreck they are working on; it has not needed to be until it became possible for all and sundry to reach the sea bottom in coastal waters. So the diver who finds something, from a spot favoured by lobsters, to a treasure ship, is likely to have his find plundered and vandalised at the earliest opportunity, as there are those hanging about just waiting to check what it is that has caught the interest of the diving club. And as yet they commit no crime, except sometimes, when somebody bothers to enforce them, against the laws of wreck, salvage and treasure trove. Some divers even make a practice of robbing the crab and lobster pots set by fishermen. No pun intended, but how low can you sink.

The great limiting factor on diving is of course weather and sea conditions. The clearest water round our coasts is off rocky shores, where even moderate weather can cause heavy swells and breaking surf. Not necessarily a deterrent to diving, but certainly uncomfortable or dangerous for small boat tenders.

A little further out off sandy or muddy shores, the water may be clear enough for pleasant diving, but currents and tides carry particles through the clear water reducing visibility especially for cameras which record everything. Strong tides also make diving difficult and dangerous as the diver is swept along with them.

In fact the conditions vary continuously with tide and weather, and perfect diving conditions may only occur a few times during a season, when you are actually able to take advantage of them. So often the only day when you can go diving turns out to be useless, and yesterday and tomorrow perfect!

Rowing

Rowing as a sport takes place in clubs all around our coasts, and although the basic techniques of oarsmanship remain the same, to row in pairs, fours or eights or individually with or without coxswains on the open sea or in open water in estuaries, can be very different from rowing upriver or on inland waters. Sculling, either singles or doubles, is where each rower has two oars, as opposed to the one oar per man (or woman) in the bigger boats.

Waves and tides affect the rower enormously, and even the difficulties of launching and recovering the fragile boats on a shingle beach when the waves are breaking, set sea rowing as a sport apart. The clubs hold regattas throughout the summer and row against each other in sections containing all the clubs on that coastline. The clubs begin training youngsters very early on, and are usually the focal point of lively social life.

Rowing as a means of moving a small boat from A to B is an essential skill and it is not very difficult, although it can be very hard work against the tide. A few minutes' instruction by someone who can row, and then a few hours practice, blisters and aching muscles, and you will be able to handle a boat with oars. Rowing with one oar, standing up and 'sculling' over the stern is also a good way of moving a small light boat around a harbour, and requires a half-circle-shaped notch in the transom in which to rest the oar, which is held at the top by both hands and worked with a kind of figure of eight movement in the water, pivoting on the transom. This propels the boat forward and with a little practice you learn to alter direction by a slight change of emphasis in your sculling.

Rowing club: emptying
the boat

If you have learned to row on a nice, smooth, park pond or river,
'feathering' your blades on the back strokes and gliding along effort-
lessly over the opaque surface, you will find it is a different matter to
row a dinghy in tidal water. Even the slightest chop makes it more
difficult and the oars must be dug more deeply into the water with a
higher hand action, and a short strong stroke, before being taken out
well clear of the water on recovery, or they will be smacking into the
wave tops all the time.

Canoeing

Modern canoeing is done in two main types of craft; the first is the
decked canoe or kayak, propelled by double-bladed paddles, usually
single seaters. They have spray covers which fit round the cockpit rim
and the canoeist's waist like a kind of sleeve, to prevent water entering

Hornet dinghy: the author in the water, temporarily *(Basil M. Kidd)*

the boat. They are never so tight that the canoeist cannot escape easily when capsized. The canoes are made of glass fibre so are easy to repair, and quite easy to make at home. The second type is the Canadian canoe, undecked, propelled with single-bladed paddles, and usually double seated. Within these two main types are many variations for various purposes. Canadian canoes for river, lake and coastal touring, roomy and stable, and slalom and racing canoes in differing kayak designs.

A canoe is a good way of getting around in shallow water, but is certainly not the safest craft. Strict rules must be obeyed, such as the wearing of lifejackets and crash helmets and in making sure your canoe has correct buoyancy. It is unwise to go alone, as a canoe cannot be righted once capsized in deep water without it becoming waterlogged and therefore useless as a life raft. Only if other canoeists are there to lift the boat right out of the water across their own canoes, can it be emptied and the crew get back in.

Canoe surfing is fun even in very light surf, but should not be tried without at least a little experience and tuition. Canoe clubs abound and really it is best to join one if you intend to be serious about the sport, which in most clubs is highly competitive. It goes without saying that before anyone ventures out in a canoe he should be a competent swimmer.

Full information about clubs, etc, can be got from The British Canoe Union. There is a national coaching scheme with courses and proficiency tests run by this union. The country is divided into areas which roughly coincide with the Sports Council regions. Ask at your local sports centre for information.

Racing Dinghies

During the last war plywood was developed for building planes, and someone soon tumbled to the obvious idea of using this much improved and cheap product for building boats. The small plywood Cadet intended for teaching youngsters to sail proved so successful that it was followed by a succession of designs progressively more sophisticated. For many years boats were cheap, but now inflation has sent costs soaring. New dinghies can cost more than £1,000, and even cheaper and secondhand boats may be out of the financial reach of many young people who form the majority of dinghy sailors and are the up and coming helmsmen of the future. The development of plastics and glass fibre has also caused a dinghy building revolution, as in all other types of boat. The inflexibility of plywood limited design to hard chine boats with a distinct angle between bottom and sides and no double curves, as plywood cannot be bent two ways at the same time, but glass fibre can be moulded to any shape whatsoever and soft chine or round-bottomed designs are again possible. In keeping with modern trends, do-it-yourself kits are available for many dinghy classes which reduces the cost a lot and keeps the plywood types going where they might otherwise be completely superseded by glass fibre.

Your choice of dinghy will be influenced by your experience of sailing, and by the classes sailed at whatever local sailing club you intend to join. Most clubs sail several classes of boat, and almost all have a fleet of Mirror dinghies. This small dinghy has been the success story of the post-war dinghy world, and rightly so, because it provides a (comparatively) cheap boat, easily built from a kit, with most of the sailing qualities of a big thoroughbred dinghy. It is easy and safe to sail and to right if it is capsized. It is light enough for youngsters to manhandle on and off the beach and trailers. It is easily repairable. It is extremely seaworthy. It is not a fast boat, but can hold its own on handicap with anything when well sailed. In tidal water its lack of

An Albacore beaching in a rough sea. The main halliard having broken, she was forced to come in too slowly and got 'dumped'

speed over the surface makes it difficult to make much headway in light airs over strong tides. It can be rowed or used with a very small outboard motor. About its only disadvantage is that in surf conditions on and off beaches, it is very light and a bit liable to get knocked back. When you graduate from a Mirror to something bigger and faster, your boat has excellent secondhand value as there are always new-comers looking for Mirrors.

A happier view of an Albacore, a family dinghy with a laminated hull

A Mirror, one of the most popular post-war dinghies

Because of the increasing cost of boats, and because of the difficulty of finding expert crews to do a lot of the work without any of the thrill of helming, singlehanded classes have increased enormously in numbers over the last few years. The success of the plywood and the fibreglass Minisail, and the glass fibre Laser, has been followed by the increasing popularity of the little wooden Streaker, good on the water and light on the beach, and the wooden Phantom, a big singlehander extremely fast but needing a strong and fairly heavy helmsman to sail it in anything but light winds. For catamaran enthusiasts there is the singlehanded Unicorn. Most clubs now have a singlehander fleet, whereas ten years ago there would only be one or two singlehanders in each club, regarded as slightly potty by the other helmsmen.

Do not, if you are a beginner, be tempted to buy any of the faster or more advanced types of boat without first having some sailing experience in all wind conditions.

The finest way to learn to sail is to crew for a season with an experienced helmsman and to persuade him to let you helm sometimes after races. A course at a holiday sailing school may teach you the basics, but does not provide much real experience. To attempt to learn to sail racing dinghies by trial and error on open water is bound to lead to trouble, even in sheltered water and in light airs. Most sailing clubs do run instruction courses, especially for junior or cadet members.

Racing dinghies are very rarely left on moorings, but are parked on trolleys or sledges.

SAILING CLUBS

These vary enormously from the family club which may have in it dinghies of half a dozen classes, and which welcomes youngsters and picnickers and potterers as well as racing, to the high-powered club which has not got much time for any but the young bloods with Olympic aspirations who hang out on trapeze wires and crash around with their spinnakers up in enormous seas and gale-force winds.

A few have motor boating, waterskiing and/or fishing sections, and while this may be fine for some, this type of club may turn out to be full of warring factions for the sports are not really compatible, and fair shares of launching ramps, winch use, club facilities, and sea room produces continual problems.

All clubs which have vacancies will welcome you, but most specify that you do sail one of their recognised classes.

Minisail with its sliding plank and *(right)* a Moth

Windsurfing

Windsurfing is the latest water sport. It developed from the discovery by owners of such singlehanded boats as Minisails that it was possible to stand up and hang on to the boom and sail the boat 'on the wind' steering it by body movements, at least for a short while, and that this was exciting and demanding even when done on smooth water rather than in enormous breakers like true surfing.

The specialist windsurfing craft has a hull based on the GRP sports surfboard already highly developed for control by body movements. On this is mounted a mast which collapses when the board capsizes, so that it can easily be righted and the mast heaved back into position. The boom is a kind of double bow which allows the surfer to lean well away from the sail and thus sail the board on a broader reach than he could by holding a straight boom.

The surfer starts with the board head to wind, pulls the boom in a little to catch the wind, at the same time steering the board slightly away from the wind with feet and body shift. The sail fills and the board moves off, and from there on it is all balance and sail control. To go about, the board is brought head to wind and the surfer nips around the front of the mast. All this takes plenty of practice and many capsizes and duckings. You must wear a wet suit and be reasonably fit, for although it is easy enough to right the board and climb back on it, each time it takes a little more out of you.

Windsurfers will travel in extremely light winds, although it takes a little breeze to put enough pressure on the sail to balance body weight and make it easier. Then as the wind gets up it all becomes extremely fast and difficult – 'hairy', to use the dinghy sailors' expression.

Fast dinghies launching for a race

The relatively calm waters of estuaries and the absence of breakers inshore makes them ideal places for this sport, and every season there are more and more of these bright-sailed butterflies about. Wear a wet suit and a lifejacket which fits neatly and is not so cumbersome that it impedes movement, and go ashore for a rest when you become tired or cold.

Power Boating

Unfortunately all too many people take power boats on to the water without knowing the rules of the road at sea, confident that with all that space, unlike a main road, it is easy to avoid accidents. They are often totally unaware of the variety of accidents that might happen or of the damage that they might do. Estuaries and coastal waters are available to all who wish to use them for any working or sporting purpose from fishing to diving for pirate's gold; there is just not the division and siting and enclosing of activities that goes on on land, and anything can be happening anywhere at the same time. Crab pots, whelk pots, longlines, moorings, sailing club racing marks and other things often with very minimal buoys as markers get laid almost anywhere and not only may they be damaged by your boat, but can also cause you serious and dangerous damage. Therefore you should always make it your business to know where fixed obstructions are and to keep an eye open for pots or lines set in differing positions. Because of the big changes in depth of tidal water, and also the changing direction of tidal flow, buoys and markers have long lines beneath them giving them plenty of 'scope' to alter their positions accordingly. At low or slack water these lines float in coils under the surface and create a dreadful hazard especially for power boats.

Study your chosen area for power boating at low tide and take note of underwater obstructions, old wrecks, jetties, rocks, lumps of concrete, etc, etc. Such obstructions are normally moved or clearly marked in any places where boating is going on, especially any commercial work, but can be a danger in odd corners of estuaries and harbours where few people would normally take a boat at all.

Keep your boat away from people fishing either from beach, pier or other boats, and from swimmers and bathing beaches. Do not 'buzz' sailing dinghies or tear through the middle of a dinghy race. In other words respect other peoples' sports and remember that they think of you and your boat as a noisy smelly nuisance. The joy of power boating belongs only to the participator, not to the spectator.

186

Never forget that a boat at speed, particularly on a turn, is exerting forces on your body which can throw you right out of the boat if you are not properly seated in it. It is very unsafe to perch on the side of the boat or on the back of a seat, and although a passenger may get no more than a ducking if thrown overboard, if the driver goes, the power boat with no one at the helm or throttle, is lethal to other people.

Never drive a boat for a water skier without also carrying an observer. This frees you to watch what is ahead of you and not be continually turning round, putting anyone or anything in your course in mortal danger. This is a rule which is all too often ignored. The laws about such things are lax in this country, but many waterski drivers would find themselves in dead trouble in other European countries or

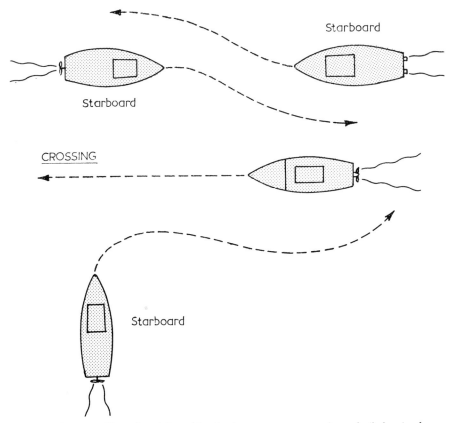

Power boat traffic rules: *(above)* both alter course to starboard; *(below)* when boats cross the boat with other boat on her starboard side must keep clear, passing astern

in Australia where the laws are very strict indeed.

Always carry an anchor big enough to hold your boat and at least 10 fathoms of anchor warp, a hooter, six parachute flares, a fire extinguisher, a good first aid kit and a couple of survival blankets as used by mountaineers and walkers which take up little room and could be invaluable, and if you use your boat for fishing, a can of fresh water and some emergency rations. Never go on the sea without a compass.

Always check that your petrol tank is full before going off on anything but a very short trip (in fact always check it). Carry a basic tool kit including new spark plugs and a starting cord if used. Just because you can get so quickly from A to B in a power boat it does not follow that you are safe not to carry emergency kit as mentioned above, properly stowed in waterproof plastic bags. Sooner or later the unexpected will happen and you will be glad of something in your kit. It only needs to be used once to be completely justified.

Obey the safety rules and regulations of any club you may belong to.

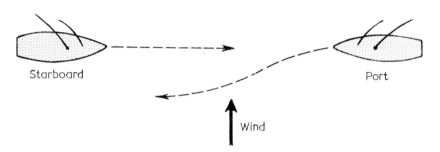

Two sailing boats meeting: boat with wind coming from starboard side has right of way

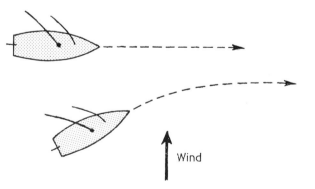

Sailing boats on same tack: boat to windward keeps clear

The rules of the road at sea are clear enough, and in harbours and estuaries there may be local river authority regulations which take precedence over them and should be studied. The main ones which apply to power boats are as follows:

1. Two power boats approaching each other head on should alter course to starboard (right), so that they pass left handed or port side. If you are approaching another boat at any distance, from any angle, and its relative bearing (to you) does not change then you are on a collision course. If it widens, *you* will pass ahead, if it narrows *he* will pass ahead.
2. When two boats on a parallel course decide to cross courses, the boat with the other boat on her right must keep clear.
3. Power must give way to sail.
4. Even though you have right of way, you must give way to avoid a collision. Never take a chance that you can just clear the bows of another boat; slacken speed and cross behind it.
5. The onus is on an overtaking boat to keep clear of the boat he is overtaking (obviously, because he is going faster so has more manoeuvrability).
6. Keep to the right in a river or narrow channel (starboard).
7. A powered vessel about to turn should indicate this as follows:
    One short blast on siren or hooter. I am altering course to starboard and turning right.
    Two short blasts. I am altering course to port and turning left.
    Three short blasts. I am going astern, backwards, in reverse.
    Five or more short blasts. Keep clear (reason unspecified). Keep it up until you have your boat under control again.
8. In a fog, sound off a long blast at frequent intervals every 20 or 30 seconds, and *slow down*.

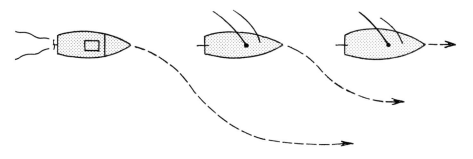

Overtaking under power or sail: the faster boat must keep clear; it has more manoeuverability and can see better

9. Keep clear of big boats, especially those moving away from harbour walls or down narrow channels. It may be that you could be sucked against their sides by the turbulence from their propellers, or could force them on to sand or mud to avoid you if you insist on your rights in a very narrow channel. Certain types of coasters do use the navigable channels of small estuaries and rivers at high tide, where there is little or no margin for error.

WATERSKIING

This is the most popular water sport for those who have power boats. There are hundreds of waterskiing clubs especially on the sheltered inshore waters of our estuaries. Refer to specialist books or your club for instruction.

It is an exhilarating and spectacular sport, but it is very unpopular with non skiers and power boaters because it can, if not done under proper control and with much consideration for all the others using the water, be destructive and dangerous. I feel that it is a case of live and let live, but that clubs and local authorities could, by defining much more strictly than is done at present, areas of water where skiing may take place, make life easier for everyone concerned. Non skiers would be far safer than they are at present and skiers could feel much freer to carry on their sport without having to worry all the time about other water users.

Skiing at its best takes place on water where no other users of any kind may encroach while skiing is in progress. This on the whole applies only to lakes, reservoirs, etc, which can easily be so controlled. On coastal water, the problems are far greater.

FURTHER READING   McDonald, Kendall. *The Underwater Book* and *The Second Underwater Book* (Pelham); Norman, K. *Modern Waterskiing* (Faber & Faber); du Cane, P. *High Speed Small Craft* (David & Charles); Dobbs, Horace. *Camera Underwater* (Focal Press); Wilmot, Bill St John. *Nautical Archaeology* (David & Charles); Hampton, T. A. *The Master Diver and Underwater Sportsman* (David & Charles); Skilling, Brian. *Canoeing Complete* (Kaye & Ward); *British Sub Aqua Club Diving Manual* (BSAC); *British Sub Aqua Club Snorkelling Manual* (BSAC); Bowyer, P. *Boat Engines* (David & Charles).

USEFUL ADDRESSES   *Royal Yachting Assen,* 5 Buckingham Gate, London SW1; *The British Water Ski Federation* and *The British Sub Aqua*

Club, both at 70 Brompton Road, London SW3; *The Hydrofoil and Multihull Society,* 113 Brunswick Road, Thorpe Bay, Essex; *The Yacht and Motor Boat Asscn,* 90 Bedford Court Mansions, Bedford Avenue, London WC1; *National Snorkellers Club,* 13 Langham Gardens, Wembley, Middx; *British Canoe Union,* 26-29 Park Crescent, London W1N 4DT.

11

Beach Law and Beachcombing

Law and the Water

RIPARIAN RIGHTS

As far upstream as the tide flows, the bed of a river belongs to the Crown and it is a public navigable river. All rivers above tidal flow are privately owned. The public may have navigation rights on such private rivers by usage or by Act of Parliament, but this gives no rights of property or fishing, only rights of way, which includes anchorage.

Riparian rights are the legal rights of a landowner in respect of a natural stream flowing through or alongside his land. If alongside, his rights extend to midstream and include the exclusive right of fishing, so that the owner alone can license others to fish there.

To find out more details about riparian rights which do not strictly affect tidal waters, check in the legal manuals in the reference section of the public library.

FORESHORE RIGHTS

The shore below high water mark is Crown Property unless the Crown has assigned it to someone else. This can be a local authority or river board, the National or some other Trust, a lord of the manor, or a private individual. No one has a right to cross an assigned foreshore or to park cars or boats or caravans or tents upon it. Foreshore controlled by local authorities is subject to their byelaws in such respects. That controlled by private individuals or others is protected by the laws of trespass in exactly the same way as any other property, and you cannot do anything without the express permission of the owners.

The ground above high water mark, mistakenly referred to as the foreshore, belongs to whoever owns the land adjoining it. In most cases no one worries very much about pedestrians using such areas unless of course they are private gardens. But the moment anyone puts

If the coast begins at the first bridge, this is the top of the Thames estuary!

up a tent or parks cars or boats, and makes pathways, then farmers, golf clubs, and other owners are perfectly entitled to enforce their rights and can take action against trespassers if any damage has been done. Rights of way frequently do exist to allow access to beaches, but should not be assumed as a matter of course.

SHOOTING

There is some confusion here. Anyone may shoot along the tideline, below the normal spring tide high water mark, between 1 September and 20 February. Nevertheless other people are also free to use the same area and one is not allowed to carry a firearm in a public place, so theoretically a shooter could be prosecuted. However, the Wildfowlers Association of Great Britain and Ireland has arranged with the Crown Commissioners, immunity for members of their own association or clubs affiliated to it, so it is important that wildfowlers do join the Association. (See page 207)

WRECK LAWS

Everything you may find on the beach except natural objects like dead seagulls, does in fact belong to someone. If it has come from a wreck (and it is not a wreck so long as a man, a cat or a dog survives upon it) the owner has a year and a day in which to lay claim to it. Otherwise it belongs to the Crown or to someone to whom the Crown has granted a 'franchise of wreck'. Wreck is classified as either 'owned' or 'unclaimed' and the finder of goods must report finds to the Receiver of Wrecks, usually the local customs officer. The coastguard will tell you where to find him. If the wreck is 'owned' then the finder may claim salvage rights from the owner, with the Receiver of Wrecks as arbiter. Interference with an owned wreck without the owner's permission may involve a fine. To remove parts of the wreck and not return them to the owner may also incur a fine.

An unclaimed wreck is entered in a register by the Receiver when reported and this process is known as 'opening a droit'. After a year and a day, if still unclaimed, it reverts to the Crown for sale, and the finder or salvor usually gets about a third of the proceeds, although this figure may vary. It depends on the value and difficulty of the salvage. Those who want to make a habit of salvage on any scale should make it their business to study and know the salvage laws. This also applies of course to skin divers doing salvage work.

Articles washed overboard, from a ship which has *not* been wrecked, are classed as lost property, and the laws for that apply. This also includes navigation marks, buoys, etc, which have gone adrift. An exception is fishing gear which if lost overboard does count as wreck, even though the fishing boat has not in fact been wrecked.

Such lost property if found and kept can be deemed to have been stolen, and you are subject to the laws of common larceny. So be a bit careful.

Flotsam, by the way, is wreck or goods found floating at sea. Jetsam has been deliberately thrown overboard. Ligan has been either thrown over and marked with a buoy or cast ashore.

Obviously it is best to report anything of any value. Valued at over £20, the find must be reported by the Receiver of Wrecks to Lloyds. Small objects may be sold by the Receiver and the proceeds go to the salvor.

The Receiver has power to enter private land if he suspects that an offence against the wreck laws has been committed. He must stop people looting a wreck, and in fact you do commit an offence if you board a wreck without the owner's or Receiver's permission.

Especially now that skin diving for treasure has become so popular, note that wrecks of possible archaeological interest must be reported to the Receiver and to the Council for Nautical Archaeology through the National Maritime Museum at Greenwich.

Beachcombing

In spite of the above-mentioned laws about objects of any value found on the beach, there is always something of interest along the tideline of any beach, neither valuable enough to rate as wreck, nor old enough to rate as archaeological. There is something fascinating about walking slowly along, head down, scanning the mess of tarry seaweed, broken plastic, bits of old rope, odd shoes, timber, old motor tyres, for the odd treasure. Your feet, which should be well shod on such occasions, scuffle through the rubbish, disturbing the flies on the rotten seaweed, and kicking occasionally at anything which might turn out to be interesting. The good beachcomber has an eye which ignores the rubbish and yet picks out in an instant anything unusual or 'likely'. He

Looking for whatever a scouring high tide might have brought

has the same qualities as the good mushroomer – walking for miles, head down, but seeing instantly whatever he is looking for. Always beachcomb down sun, so that the cast shadows are away from you and the objects stand out in good relief.

There is all mankind's rubbish to be found, and some of man's work turned by the sea and sand into things far more interesting, and occasionally bits and pieces which might actually come in useful. Beware, however, of any unopened cans or containers. Check to see if there are numbers or identification letters, and do *not* open such things unless they are quite definitely just tins of paint. The larger the container, up to oil drum size, the better it is to leave it alone and report it to the coastguard.

Pieces of boat which have obviously not been in the sea very long, should also be reported in case they provide a clue to boats lost at sea, or even stolen from moorings or dinghy parks.

Various types of drift markers are released periodically by the people responsible for oceanographic surveys, chart markings, etc, and these always carry instructions to the finder as to where they should be returned with details of where found.

Occasionally shells, bullets, bombs, landmines, mortar bombs, unexploded flares, and dangerous objects of that kind appear. Most of them are relics from the war, probably long covered over and now uncovered by changing beach configuration. These can still be lethal and liable to go off if disturbed. Such finds should be left well alone and reported to the police or coastguard.

Especially on shingle beaches, where summer visitors lie around, money can be found after certain tides. Money which falls out of pockets slips downwards through the shingle until it reaches the firm bed at the bottom. There it stays until wild winds and scouring tides pull away loose shingle and expose the hard bed, and after storms there will be plenty of beachcombers of all ages out along the banks looking for loot.

In certain areas, coal can be found on the beach, and for some hard work, hundredweights gathered for winter use. In some places such as Easington on the Northumberland coast, this coal is washed out of pit waste tipped along the beach, but in others it just appears, particularly after storms. There are exposed seams of coal underwater from which the rough sea breaks it loose. This soft coal comes ashore to be gathered or breaks up very quickly to grit and dust.

Beach timber burns well enough although the salt in it makes it spit and produce pretty flames. However, wet wood is hard to saw up, and heavy to carry, and should be piled where it can dry out. If it has come from wrecks or from old piers and jetties, then it may be full of nails, bolts and screws, and very dangerous to tackle with any kind of power saw, but the timbers washed over the side from the deck cargoes of coasters, and pallets which have been heaved overboard, provide a very useful source of usable timber. Beach timber is usually hardwood, softwood breaks up and splinters too easily in rough seas and marine borers get into it and riddle it with holes.

Natural wood, bits of tree trunk and branch, and old worm-riddled timbers, weathered into interesting shapes, look fine as part of fancy flower arrangements or even to make unusual lamp standards, but on the whole salt-soaked timber does not dry out well enough to be of lasting use. Big pieces which still have some heartwood in good condition may be of some use, but all soft and rotten wood must be pared and cut away. Then leave it out in the rain and wind for a few months, before letting it dry naturally and again working on the wood to reach a sound surface which can be sanded and waxed.

SHELLS

Although there are millions of shells on every shore, they are very fragile and the absolutely perfect specimen which is worth collecting or using, is quite hard to find. Seashells, like pebbles, look lovely when wet and washed, but tend to be very dull when dried out. A coat of clear varnish will bring up the colours, but be sure that the shells have first been thoroughly washed in fresh water. Even when scoured by the sea, and fresh water, seashells tend to smell dreadful after a while unless absolutely clean.

The first shell which I learned to identify was the cowrie, in its European version a little shell up to a quarter of an inch long, pink, creamy, or lilac, with whorls round it like fingerprints, found in the sandy shingle of North Devon beaches, where the rocks ended. These we collected and took home to be used as 'counters' when we played cards, valued at twelve for a penny; they were convenient currency. I still collect these cowries along the tidelines at Sandwich Bay where they can be found in profusion mixed with little pieces of coal and other light rubbish left as the tide recedes over the sand. When we used them as currency I did not know that other types of cowrie, to be found in different sizes and colours all over the world, were known as 'money shells' and actually used as currency in some parts of the Pacific.

On our beaches one cannot find anything huge and exciting in the way of shells, such as I have picked up on the beaches of New Zealand, but nevertheless the variety is considerable, and the colours and configurations delicate and beautiful, and there never seem to be any two shells exactly alike (except the two halves of a bivalve).

Collecting shells can be an expensive hobby, as there are shell dealers who will, at a price, supply anything from anywhere in the world.

If you are collecting bivalves – shells of any shape which are in two halves – tie the two halves together with thread immediately you pick up the shell, or it will surely break into its two parts before you get it home as the hinges are weak.

SEAWEED

The Victorians collected seaweed and made pictures, some quite attractive, which turn up in sale rooms occasionally. Collect only fresh seaweed, not the stuff already dried out on the beach. Put it in shallow bowls of sea water and clean it carefully with a large, soft, watercolour brush. Then slip a piece of mounting card under the seaweed and lift it to the surface, tease it into position with the paintbrush or a knitting needle, and lift it clear. Lay the whole thing on a piece of botanical drying paper, white blotting paper, or even newspaper, and cover it with another piece. Lay a heavy book on top and leave to dry. The seaweed will adhere to the card.

To clean seaweed for picture making, wash it in fresh water and carefully lay out the pieces on card by hand while still wet, before drying as above. The weed will dry out in the shapes and positions you have arranged, but lacking so much salt, they may not stick, and can be held in place with a little wallpaper adhesive applied carefully with a brush.

PEBBLES

There are millions and millions of tons of pebbles round our coasts; pebbles which come in the main from the cliffs and banks of great geological diversity, washed out by the sea. Chalk, for instance, contains great nodules of flint, and there are always many flint stones beneath our chalk cliffs. These pebbles move constantly with the tides, and drift constantly in the direction of the prevailing currents of particular localities, which cause the waves to move obliquely in to the beach. The size of the pebbles dictates how far along beaches they will be carried by normal sea conditions, and this produces a grading of sizes on beaches of any length. The most famous example of this is the

Chesil Bank. From Bridport in the west to the Isle of Portland in the east, a distance of 17 miles, the pebbles range from pea-sized pellets to 6in stones. It is said that a local, landing on the beach in a fog, can tell exactly whereabouts he is by the size of the stones. Experiments with broken bricks, which were scattered at random along the beach, proved most interesting. In due course each piece of brick, showing up well among the pebbles, found its way to its appropriate size area and settled down to enjoy a peaceful co-existence with its pebble peers.

The force of gales and heavy seas allied with spring and neap tides, continually changes the profile of a shingle beach. Big storms sometimes scour away huge masses of stones and deposit them elsewhere, or build up great high ridges which persist for many years until even greater storms move them again.

Another unbelievable deposit of shingle is the huge spit of Dungeness. Mostly of flint pebbles with some sandstone and quartzite, the ness has been built up over centuries by the oblique movement of south-westerly winds up the channel forming fulls (banks) and swales (valleys), out to the point of the ness. The shingle which goes round this corner is then piled back on the easterly coast by the north-easterly winds coming down the channel. The ness points at France, and the channel is not very wide here. Winds from the south and south east are not usually very strong and do not pile up enough heavy seas to disperse the shingle. Only in an aerial photograph can one see the fantastic complexity of ridges and valleys made by the sea in such a place, formations which still inexorably continue, in spite of nuclear power station and the like. In spite of local advice about this continual shifting of the shingle, the nuclear power station is too near the western side of the spit, and there is a fleet of lorries which do nothing but pick up shingle from the western side and dump it back on the east, so as to maintain the status quo.

Any and every pebble is interesting, and if you have a polisher can be made beautiful if it is not already. Semi-precious stones can be found, jet from the Yorkshire coast round Whitby, and amber on the Norfolk coast. Amber is not strictly a stone, being fossilised resin from antediluvian forests, but in the beachcombers' books ranks as such. Cornelian or carnelian abounds on the Norfolk coast in small pieces, and I spent hours as a child hunting for it. I think that was how I developed my beachcomber's 'eye', picking out the bright red translucent pieces from the browns and ochres of the other pebbles. Any and every pebble beach be it miles long or just a patch of shingle may yield beautiful and interesting stones, semi-precious or otherwise;

banded agate, granite, sandstone, onyx, and many others. Not just those from the cliffs and rocks behind them, but stones washed along for many miles by the prevailing currents along our beaches.

Stone polishers are tumblers worked electrically, into which you place your stones, with emery powder and water. They make a bit of a racket, and it takes many hours to polish a stone properly. You will also need a stone saw with which to slice and cut your pebbles to reveal the internal patterns and layering.

FURTHER READING   Soper, Tony. *The Shell Book of Beachcombing* (David & Charles); Barret and Yonge. *The Collins Pocket Guide to the Seashore* (Collins); Dance, P. *The Shell Collector's Guide* (David & Charles); Ellis, C. *The Pebbles on the Beach* (Faber); Evans, I. O. *The Observer's Book of Sea and Seashore* (Warne); Forsyth, W. *Common British Seashells* (A. & C. Black); Charles, Barry. *Discovering Seashells* (Shire); Deeson, A. F. L. (ed.) *The Collector's Encyclopaedia of Rocks and Minerals* (David & Charles).

12

Birds

There are so many varieties of birds to be seen on and near the coast. There are the birds of saltmarsh and estuary, waders, ducks, geese, swans; birds of sea and seashore, cormorants, seagulls and more waders; birds of rocky cliffs, gannets, guillemots, puffins; and all the migrant land birds passing in and out.

The openness of estuaries and seashore make it possible, with the aid of binoculars, to see the birds so much more easily than inland, and they are usually in groups or flocks. Because they also can see clearly, they feel safe and allow a fairly close approach. If you are working on the seashore, the birds come closer and closer, searching for any food which you may disturb, and the less notice you appear to take of them, the bolder they become. Many birds nest in traditional (for them) nesting sites year after year and are always protected by law, but nevertheless some of these sites can be carefully approached and the experience of a ternery or gannet rock in nesting time is overwhelming.

Armed with binoculars and a good bird book, you can of course be a solitary bird watcher, but bird watchers, like the creatures they study, seem to like to form groups and societies, and these abound in all areas. The advantage of joining a club or society is that it is usually led by a knowledgeable ornithologist who always takes a responsible attitude, not disturbing nests or interfering with birds in any way. Clubs are usually affiliated to one or other of the main ornithological societies.

Depending on how involved you wish to become, your bird watching may take various forms: observation for its own sake, photography, or census work. Much counting goes on all the time and is largely done by members of local ornithological societies. The Seabird Group carried out a long and complex census and survey of the twenty-four species of seabird known to nest in this country and

Seagull tracks in the mud

produced a definitive book on the subject. Especially in view of the enormous damage done to bird populations of sea and coast by oil pollution and other even more insidious kinds of pollution, the continuing study of birds is extremely useful as a guide to what is happening in the oceans of the world upon which mankind in the long run depends.

Bird Recognition

This is not as easy as it might seem. Various authors in various books have tried to classify birds visually for ease of identification, but no one has yet come up with the really perfect answer. There are variations of colour and size, and the occasional bird nests right out of its normal habitat, or appears where it should not be at that time. Fleeting glimpses through binoculars can also be very misleading. Sometimes birds in immature or winter plumage bear little resemblance to the adult bird. There are so many splendidly illustrated books on the market that it would be invidious to name any particular one. Each has its sections on birds of specialist habitat, and gives full details of plumage, breeding and migratory habits. Study the illustrations in bird books and memorise as many as possible, and then a day will come when you see a bird that is unfamiliar but which you can recognise. For instance, having memorised it, you will know that the only black and white wader with an upturned bill and bright pale blue legs is an avocet. It is much more difficult to identify some of the indiscriminate brown birds of all sizes which abound, but each does have perhaps one distinctive feature, of plumage, bill or size. The search for rare species is of course always fascinating, yet so is the study of the huge flocks of birds which abound in some places, especially of waders, ducks, etc, at certain times of the year.

First Aid

Unfortunately, birds which have got oil on them are very hard to save, and one which is seriously oiled should be put out of its misery. Apart from the clogging of feathers it may well have poisoned itself by trying to clean up with its beak and thus ingesting oil. Kill small birds with a quick twist of the neck, and large birds by hitting them hard at the base of the skull. Not for the squeamish, but any vet or local RSPCA man will do the job. The RSPCA give advice about cleaning oil-clogged birds and it is sometimes possible to clean them if they are only slightly oiled. The difficulty is to keep them alive until the next moult when new feathers will replace the spoiled ones. Occasionally it may be possible to release them right away, but only if they fly properly and can look after themselves, and of course don't release them back into a still polluted sea. Seabirds will have to be given fish and sea water, and may have to be force fed. Really it is a most difficult job unless you are prepared to give a lot of time and patience to it.

One occasionally finds a seabird which has taken a fishing line or got snagged on the hook. There is usually little to do except kill the bird, although occasionally a vet may be able to get a hook out. Seagulls do take bait from the water, but the main cause of trouble is baited hooks left lying about by careless beach fishermen, or traces which have broken in the water by becoming snagged, and have then been exposed at low tide for the birds to get at.

Birds with damaged wings can be saved if the damage is near the tip. The primary feathers can be cut short and the bird thus pinioned so that it cannot fly till the next moult. If it can be kept properly fed, the

Fulmers *(John Marchington)*

wing may mend and the bird survive. Broken legs below the knee joint can be splinted with small slips of wood and adhesive tape, but breaks high up mean that the bird must be destroyed. One frequently sees one-legged seagulls, perhaps with a leg hanging in flight which the bird is unable to retract. Such a big bird may be able to survive with one leg, especially a species which spends more time at sea than on land, provided it can swim and take off effectively with only one leg.

Shot wounds may be only superficial, and pellets should be carefully picked out and the wounds gently dabbed with cotton wool and warm water. Serious gunshot wounds cannot be dealt with and the bird should be destroyed. It will probably have several pellets far too deep to be removable.

Large seabirds can be very difficult to control and don't want to be helped! Seagulls have vicious hooked beaks and can inflict unpleasant wounds. Throw a blanket or sack over the bird until you can control it properly. Grasp it firmly round the base of the wings, above the back, and hold long-necked birds just behind the head with the other hand so that they cannot reach round and peck you. Ducks and small birds will usually stay on their backs if placed in that position, either in the hand or on a table, and any way you can black-out a bird makes it calmer as it thinks night has fallen. Put the head in a bag, but not an airtight polythene or paper bag, or it will suffocate.

The RSPCA will usually tell you if there is a local expert in such matters, and there very often is.

One occasionally finds exhausted birds. If these are racing pigeons bearing rings, which have just come to land after crossing water, all they may need is a rest, a drink of water, and a bit of seed or corn before flying on. Weather conditions may sometimes catch migrant flocks and force the exhausted birds to land; there is little one can do unless the birds are seed eaters. Insectivorous birds are doomed as one cannot supply their needs. Recently the Europe-bound house martins from south-east England met a gale halfway across the Channel and got blown back after fighting the wind till they could fly no longer, and they fell and died in their thousands. It may be possible to keep a seed eater alive with bird seed and water till it can fly again.

Winter Visitors

Although we may think our winter weather to be unbearably wet, windy and cold, for many winter birds, when winter grips their summer homelands, these islands, nestling cosily in the warm Gulf Stream, are a kind of package-deal holiday resort. Here we have comparatively little snow, dense population (consider central Russia) and its consequent free food supply, woodland and hedgerow shelter, and unfrozen water (consider Greenland or Iceland). So as the swallows and many other summer visitors prepare to move south with the sun, in come the big ocean-flying birds from the far north, and in stages the smaller songbirds, less able to withstand the long ocean crossings, come down through Europe to make the short hop across the Straits of Dover or the North Sea. Many smaller duck also prefer the open water to the deep, frozen lakes of central Europe.

Probably the best known winter visitor of all is the starling. These birds come in millions from Russia and the Baltic countries to join those few who like it here all the time. They arrive on the Norfolk coast like locusts and flop exhausted all over the fields and towns, before the survivors continue on to their roosts in woodlands or on the ledges of buildings in cities. Country dwellers are familiar with the flocks of starlings returning to roost as dusk falls, and if you trouble to take a compass bearing on their flight line, go 5 miles away in your car

Oyster catchers (*John Marchington*)

and take another bearing on another flock and mark on a map where the bearings cross, you will without difficulty find the main roost. This is an incredible sight. All round Trafalgar Square in London, they perch at dusk on the leeward side of the buildings, and you can hear them above the noise of the traffic. Also very common are fieldfares and redwings, usually in flocks. These too come from Northern Europe, and at first glance can be mistaken for other thrushes. The fieldfare is, however, slightly larger, slimmer and more slaty grey than the song thrush, and the redwing has a most definite patch of crimson red on each wing. Their tendency to remain in flocks, although redwings frequently nip about on lawns looking for food by themselves, does help to distinguish them from our not so gregarious resident thrushes.

Lots of European birds, such as the blackbird, normally resident anyway, also migrate here in winter to swell the population, so are more common in winter. Smaller birds loose body heat rapidly, so most come south. Others are the brambling, robin, golden plover, skylark, curlew, meadow pipit, chaffinch and lapwing.

Brent geese *(John Marchington)*

Greylags under a stormy sky *(RSPB and John Marchington)*

Many species of duck, geese and waterbirds are far more common here in the winter months. These include teal, pintail, tufted duck, widgeon, pochard, white-fronted goose, whooper swan, knot, goldeneye, coot, brent goose, barnacle goose, pinkfeet goose, Lapland bunting, sanderling, turnstone, little stint, bar-tailed godwit and ruff. Many of these birds stay in our coastal waters, returning to land when bad weather blows up, and to feed upon stubble and fresh plough. Others, such as the bar-tailed godwit, migrate here quite early in the year, go north to nest in the summer, and return here to winter with their families. Others come here in late summer and autumn, and if the winter is mild, don't bother to move on, but will, if the winter in the north and east is severe, move gradually westwards, even so far as across the sea to Ireland.

Saltmarshes, tidal estuaries, open beach and dunes, provide the most wonderful bird watching. Those who go wildfowling at first light with gun or camera, or bait digging when the tide is ebbing at dawn, see these birds in fantastic flocks; low flights of waders moving along the tideline, and parties of great whooper swans working the mudflats and flying startling white against the grey sea and wild sky.

Wildfowling

Coastal wildfowling for duck or geese is a winter sport, and a lonely one, and involves long hours, usually at dusk or dawn out in the cold and wet and in all weathers, and for the addict is the finest sport of all. He may have a companion, but is frequently alone, apart from his dog, and success is achieved by patience, knowledge and endurance, as well as by being a good shot. The size of the bag is the least important factor. Wildfowling on mudflats, saltings and foreshores involves knowing a great deal about the terrain and the habits of the many species of duck and geese. A novice should never go wildfowling without an experienced companion, and should always carry a compass. Ignorance of local conditions, tides, etc, can lead to disaster.

Anyone may shoot along the tideline below normal spring tide high water mark, between 1 September and 20 February. Nevertheless others are also free to use the same areas and one is not allowed to carry a firearm in a public place, so could theoretically be prosecuted. However, the Wildfowlers Association of Great Britain and Ireland has arranged with the Crown Commissioners immunity from such prosecution for their members or members of clubs affiliated to it, so it is important that you join the association. The spring tide limit does of course include many areas of saltmarsh and estuary which are below that limit. Nowadays many of these areas or parts of them are bird sanctuaries of various kinds, and the greatest care should be taken not to interfere with these in any way.

In the old days the wildfowler was either a local man or someone so keen that he might have come from a long way for the chance of sport. The local man would be shooting for the pot or to sell for a living, perhaps using a puntgun mounted in a long punt in which he would lie flat and paddle quietly towards a flock of feeding birds, hoping with endless patience to get near enough to fire his gun, which was a tube loaded with assorted small pieces of metal, lethal at short range, into a tightly packed flock of birds. The visitor would arrive, and lodge in a cottage or a local pub, to go out on the marshes by himself if he knew them well, or with a wildfowler who would be expert on the local tides, knowing the creeks like the back of his hand, and by long experience knowledgeable about flight lines of duck and geese and likely feeding places.

Awakening on a bitter winter morning to get up out of a warm bed long before light, to drink scalding tea and eat a plateful of porridge, to dress in the warmest possible clothes, and go out into the windy dark with gun and dog, requires considerable strength of character and purpose, and if no birds come you are frozen and miserable long

Widgeon jumping at full tide *(RSPB and Pamela Harrison)*

Pintail duck (*John Marchington*)

before it is time to go home. But if the birds come, then it is a different matter, and the excitement not only of the shooting but of the sight and sound of the birds in moonlight or dawn, and the winter dawn coming over the saltings, is worth all the agony. It never leaves you, and the wildfowler for the rest of his days keeps memories which can be stirred in a moment by the cry of flighting duck or geese wherever he may be. It is not surprising that so many wildfowlers are also painters and that many of them in the long run, shoot less and less and watch and record more and more.

Nowadays all too many people with guns, not dignified by the name of wildfowler, prowl along the shorelines and marshes shooting everything that moves, regardless of species, eating qualities, or even time of year. A groundsman at my local golf club shot two geese on the first fairway one recent cold winter, and a gaggle of twenty-seven brent geese which arrived on the East Kent coast, was reduced to five in just a few weeks. Wildfowling can be all too much like some rough shooting, carried out without regard for the birds or the animals by trigger-happy morons who nevertheless keep within the letter of the law. Any reader who is seriously interested in wildfowling should contact the Association mentioned above, and also check with local conservationists; they will put you in touch with those who engage in the sport responsibly, rather than let you cause them any trouble, even if they do try to put you off altogether.

FURTHER READING   Fitter, and Richardson. *British Birds* and *Nests and Eggs* (Collins); Fitter. *Guide to Bird Watching* (Collins); Richards, Alan. *British Birds* (David & Charles); *Book of British Birds* (Drive Publications); Cramp, Bourne, and Saunders. *The Seabirds of Britain and Ireland* (Collins); Hastings, MacDonald. *How to Shoot Straight* (Pelham); Ruffer, J. E. M. *The Art of Good Shooting* (David & Charles); Stamford, J. K. *The Complex Gun* (Pelham); Marchington, J. *The Practical Wildfowler* (A. & C. Black).

USEFUL ADDRESSES   *Wildfowlers Association of Great Britain and Ireland,* Marford Mill, Rossett, Clwyd LL12 0HL; *The Royal Society for the Protection of Birds,* Sandy, Beds; *The British Ornithologists Union* and *The Zoological Society of London,* Regents Park, London NW1 4RY; *The British Trust for Ornithology,* Beech Grove, Tring, Herts; *The Wildfowl Trust,* New Ground, Slimbridge, Glos; *The Seabird Group,* Zoology Dept, Tillydrone Avenue, Aberdeen AB9.

13

Photography

The camera can be used purely to record, but at its best is a tool with which a good photographer can create magnificent pictures, provided he is prepared to master camera and darkroom techniques. Yet however wonderful the photograph is never quite reaches the quality of a really great painting. Partly because all paintings, even water-colours, are three dimensional in that the surface of paint, canvas or paper do create texture which enhances the picture, which photo-graphic reproduction does not do, but mainly because a painting does come entirely from the eye, mind and hands of the painter, who acts as a catalyst and changes the facts of light, line and colour as they pass through him, thus imposing more of himself on a picture than a photographer can ever do.

Frank Meadow Sutcliffe's wonderful photographs taken in and around Whitby in the late nineteenth century, are enjoying a great vogue. At the time photographic techniques were very difficult, and Sutcliffe's eye for a maritime picture and his composition are unsur-passed, but I venture to say that had he been using modern cameras and modern materials, some of the pictures he produced would lack their fantastic atmosphere. The inability of film at that time to record much detail in dark areas of photos taken against the light produced a wonderful effect as in the photograph reproduced here. Sutcliffe knew this, exaggerated it in the darkroom, and so used it because he was a camera artist.

There are endless subjects for photography on or by the water, whether your interest is in boats which are all photogenic, or birds which are difficult, or the changing light and colours of sea and estuary. So many people put away their camera for the winter months, a season when the light is often at its most dramatic. There is never a day, never a time when there is nothing to photograph.

Buy the best camera that you can afford. A 35mm single lens reflex is the most convenient type for out-of-door work, and built-in focusing and light metering through the lens makes it easy to use. The more expensive modern cameras have automatic exposure control which by computer sets the shutter speed necessary, in relation to the chosen aperture setting, for a correct exposure. The very latest can also be set to a required exposure (perhaps a fast one to record movement such as bird flight) and will then compute and set the appropriate aperture setting to allow correct exposure.

Perhaps the biggest advantage of these automatic cameras is that they require little manual manipulation even when filters are used for ·black and white work, so that cold and clumsy fingers do not matter so much. For colour photography where exposure times are critical, success rate should be much higher when using an automatic camera.

The standard lens for a 35mm camera is a 50 or 55mm which gives an undistorted picture at a reasonable frame size. For wide-angle work a 35mm lens is fine. Out of doors this takes wide panoramic views but reduces the scale drastically, rather like looking through the wrong end of field glasses. Telephoto lenses do the opposite, narrowing the angle of vision or width of the picture, but magnifying the object being photographed as do field glasses the right way round. Lenses can be bought at various focal lengths and the amount of magnification needed rather depends on what you wish to photograph. For birds, except from a hide very close to the bird, a 1,000mm lens is necessary to bring it into close up; a 300mm which is a convenient size for most telephoto work will only bring birds into close up if they are around 15 yards away in the first place.

Zoom lenses are available and are variable from standard to tele-photo up to 300 or 400mm. The trouble with these is that one needs time to focus and frame up the picture in the viewfinder; this is fine for static subjects, but not so good for moving ones. The bigger the lens, the more critical the focusing tends to be, even when using small apertures to widen the depth of field. Also the bigger the lens the more difficult it is to hold the camera steady as the leverage of the long lens unbalances the camera body. There are two aids to help with this problem: a pistol grip which supports the long lens and fits on the user's arm, or a monopod. The latter as its name implies, is a single telescopic pole with a spiked or rubber foot and camera screw on the top. The camera is carried attached to the top of the closed pole and to use it you simply pull out the telescopic part as far as needed to put the camera at eye level, plant it on the ground and hold it firmly with one hand, manipulating the camera controls with the other. The camera can be angled in any direction to some extent by swinging the pole around or by using a universal joint between monopod and camera. A monopod eliminates almost all camera shake and is a lot less cumbersome than a tripod. Nevertheless for completely static work a good tripod is of course unbeatable.

Cameras are extremely susceptible to sand and water, especially salt water, and even though apparently wiped dry immediately after getting wet, in time the damage will declare itself. I had to replace a rusted shutter mechanism which was diagnosed as salt water damage, which went two years after the camera got just a little spray on it.

Special cases are available for use at sea and if you are really going to put your camera at continual risk then the expense of such a case would be justified. A most effective temporary waterproof case may be made from a plastic bag. Use a good strong plastic bag just big enough to hold the camera and cut a hole in one side to fit the back of your lens hood. Slip the camera into the bag, screw on the lens hood and then tape the bag to the back of the lens hood with Sellotape and tape up the open end of the bag. The camera controls can be worked through the plastic, but this system has the disadvantage that should you wish to change filters or film, then you will have to take the bag off and start all over again with a new one. A supply of such bags with a hole ready cut, and a roll of Sellotape should solve this problem.

Also available is an excellent sand- and water-proof camera carrying bag for outdoor use and in bad weather. In bright yellow or black this is made with inflatable sides like a lifejacket, and a zip top over a roll-down sealed opening. In this 'Sima sports pouch' the camera remains fully protected and even if it falls in the water it will float. It holds a 35mm camera and extra lenses and film, if not a full outfit of equipment. The inflated sides also act as shock absorbers and protect the delicate camera mechanism from accidental bangs and bumps.

FILM

The choice of film is very much an individual matter. If you wish to take black and white pictures and use filters to gain contrasting sky and sea and cloud effects, then fairly fast film (400 ASA) allows more latitude in poor light conditions, although medium-speed film around 125 ASA produces slightly less grainy negatives. For colour transparencies very fast film is suitable for some specialist work but it never seems to be quite so trustworthy as far as colour rendition is concerned as medium-speed films, so leave the very fast colour film to the expert. Very slow film, although it may produce colour shots large as life and twice as natural in good sunny weather, needs such long exposures in dull weather that it is difficult to use for anything but static subjects. Medium-speed film such as Agfa CT18 (64 ASA) or Kodachrome 64, are fine for most outdoor work. Agfa is especially good on blues, but may produce pictures which are slightly too blue for some. Kodachrome produces extremely well balanced transparencies. Colour is so much a matter of personal taste – and I believe that everyone sees it slightly differently – that there is no 'best' film.

As for colour-positive photography and Polaroid photography, this is such an expensive way to take photographs that it is not often used for outdoor work, except once again for specialist subjects. Colour positives do not match transparencies for reproducing light and colour, and projecting slides on to a screen with a very bright white light gives them far more quality than positives ever achieve. Colour printing in books and calendars and posters is done from transparencies by special processes not available to amateur photographers.

SUBJECTS

The wide and sometimes comparatively featureless panoramas of sea and saltmarsh do not lend themselves to black and white photography unless there is some definite feature such as a boat in the foreground. Filters to enhance sky and cloud contrasts do help a lot; yellow/orange filters do this effectively and even an ultraviolet which is colourless and so does not increase exposure times, does by cutting out some ultraviolet light increase sky contrasts.

On the other hand the magnificent variations of colour and light in these places make wonderful colour transparencies even if these are for personal showing and contemplation rather than family viewing. Boats of all kinds are very photogenic, but are always best photographed from low down, as near as possible as you can get to them, as a water-level viewpoint gives much more the impression of towering sails and foaming bow waves.

14

Seaside Houses and Houseboats

Houses by the Sea

As so many small ports declined, and as longshore fishing became relatively unprofitable, and as sailing barges and small sailing traders no longer came into our estuaries and rivers, so the homes of their people, and the other buildings associated with them, fell empty.

No need for warehouses when lorries deliver the goods regularly by road, no need for boatyards or sail-lofts, for just a handful of longshore fishing boats. No need for cottages when there are no boatmen or boatbuilders to live in them. In all the nicest places, most of those buildings and cottages have been bought up and converted either for permanent or holiday living. Sometimes this has happened to such an extent that the local people have tried hard to stop the influx of outsiders which pushes up house prices to such an extent that the locals can no longer afford to live in their own villages.

There are some half-deserted remote seaside villages where houses can still be bought cheaply, but these by their very remoteness do not attract people. Although prices go up all the time it is possible to find cottages or commercial buildings, or even boathouses, substantial enough and in good enough condition to be convertible. Of course planning permission is always necessary, and like everything else, conversion costs have skyrocketed so that it usually costs almost as much as building a new house. The advantages are that planning permission is sometimes easier to get for a conversion than for building a new house, because the kind of site one would choose to build on, beside a harbour or an estuary, probably would not get planning permission now that, quite rightly, development except in building estates and enclaves, is not encouraged, whereas converting and preserving an existing building especially if it is old and pictur-esque, is looked upon with favour. Cottages built of local stone or

Not many of these houseboats are left even in *David Copperfield* territory

flint, even if they have to be pretty well gutted inside, are ruggedly built, and blend with the countryside much better than houses made of modern materials.

A large warehouse, granary, sail-loft, boatbuilders' yard, or boat-house, may give a lot of scope for conversion to a home with big rooms and wide windows, whereas fishermen's cottages almost always have small rooms, and even knocking two into one may not make them spacious. It really depends on what you want.

Do have any building checked by a surveyor before you buy it. There may be great problems with damp as described below. Build-ings which have much timber and weather-boarding, especially if they have not been used for sometime or are layered with paint or tar, should be very carefully checked indeed for soundness and damp. What may look fine from the outside may be attached to timber framing in bad condition especially at joints, mortices and along sills. Window and door frames are particularly vulnerable.

MAINTENANCE

The maintenance of houses by the sea presents some problems not known to owners of town houses, especially where they are exposed to sea winds and are near enough to sand or salt water for it to be carried by the wind on to the house, or where there is a possibility of flooding. One only has to look at old maps to see how huge areas have become eroded away or, on the other hand, from which the sea has receded to realise that the coastline changes continually, in spite of sea walls, dredging, drainage and groynes.

When I was a child I remember being taken to see the houses falling over the cliff at Overstrand and Mundesley on the north Norfolk coast, and being horrified by the sight of gas pipes and water mains ending in thin air above piles of rubble on the beach below. Beeston Bump at Sheringham, a hill on the cliffs which went down and up again before it ended in cliffs, now only goes halfway down, and the houses built behind it when I was young, are at least a hundred yards nearer the cliff's edge and dissolution. Yet a few miles up the coast at Cley and Blakeney, the sea has receded out of sight beyond saltmarsh and sandpit and what were in medieval times active ports, are now not ports at all, or just yachting harbours. Yet in the 1953 North Sea surge Cley was flooded to a depth of 5ft and every house in the main part of the village was thoroughly soaked with salt water. Most of these houses are built of Norfolk flints and mortar with brick quoins. The salt soaked so thoroughly into the mortar that even now, twenty-six years later, it still comes out into the plaster on the inside walls of the rooms, as it hygroscopically soaks up atmospheric moisture.

Pinmill, Suffolk, where the sea comes up to the walls of the pub

This highlights one of the major problems of shoreside houses which have once been flooded by salt water. Salt remains in the walls when they have dried out and just cannot be got rid of. It appears as crystals on the surface where it can be brushed off, but will continue to do this almost indefinitely and any kind of surfacing placed directly upon it and in contact with it will eventually become damp and discoloured. In very mild cases paint the whole interior wall, when it is at its driest and cleanest, with a silicone waterproof paint, and then put on sheet polystyrene foam such as 'Warmawall'. This will keep back the moisture sufficiently for the final surface to be papered. In anything but very mild cases there is no answer but to build a wall of some kind in front of the existing wall to make a cavity, so that the salt cannot cross and the damp will evaporate away in the airspace in the cavity. Do this by battening out with wooden battens which have been thoroughly treated with waterproofing dressing or paint, on to which plasterboard or other surfacing can be fixed and decorated. Thistle-bonding, by which plasterboard is set on blobs of mortar, may result in the salt and damp crossing the mortar into the plasterboard, and is not to be recommended on salt-damp walls. Local builders are usually very aware of the problems of salt damp in walls and can advise you.

On the outside walls of houses anywhere where they are subject to occasional slight flooding, it has always been the practice to paint the lower 2 or 3 feet of the wall with black bitumen paint or tar. Modern water-resistant paints and sealers may do a better job; take the advice of local builders on this.

The specialised exterior cement-based paints, over waterproof undercoating, developed by several manufacturers, are of great value for protecting the outside walls of houses on all kinds of surfaces. Seaside houses always relied upon the very materials with which they were built, usually flint or stone, to resist the elements, for no known paint or colour wash would protect them. In some areas the walls would be hung with slate shingles very firmly attached and even cemented down.

The timber of seaside houses is vulnerable; windowsills and frames, doors and door frames, and paint, especially in certain colours, particularly blues, have never been very resistant to the salt in the air near the sea, and exterior paintwork needs to be redone more frequently than on inland houses. International Paints have developed a new clear primer which is absolutely excellent for preparing woodwork which is likely to be exposed to bad weather conditions, for painting with modern paints. However, this can only be used success-fully on new wood, or on wood from which absolutely every vestige of old paint and primer has been removed, deep into the timber.

The most important factor when redecorating exterior woodwork is the preparation and priming of the wood. Remove all old paint, and fill all gaps thoroughly, and prime the surface properly. The final paint skin must be smooth and unbroken for otherwise windblown sand and salt water will enter every tiny crack and crevice and lift and flake the paint – sand blasting is after all the best way to remove old paint, and it happens naturally to houses near sand dunes or sandy beaches. Modern yacht paints, specially the two-can mixtures, are extremely hard, and although expensive have their uses where woodwork is exposed to extreme weather conditions.

Houses nestling by the sea, bathed in summer sunshine, may look impregnable, but when continuously vicious gales batter and pound, driving rain and salt spray into every crevice, then it is a very different matter. Roofs particularly, must be sound and solid. Tiles which hang by a couple of nails and have spaces between which the wind can push brutal hands, are useless. On the west coast where the west winds across the Atlantic blow almost constantly for months, the flat slates are usually cemented in place. Pantiles, laid absolutely flat, provided they are properly anchored, do not allow wind to penetrate and lift, and interlocking tiles with the gaps cemented up can be fine where the weather is not utterly violent. Chimneys must be short and sound, and cowls or caps are necessary to prevent vicious down-draughts of wind. If your television aerial must be attached to the chimney, be sure that the chimney can take it and that the aerial is firmly put up. Use an indoor aerial if it is at all possible to get reasonable reception that way.

The doors of seaside houses should not face the prevailing wind or the sea, but should ideally be at the side or the back where they can be opened and entered in at least some shelter. A good solid porch, wherever the door is, with its door at a different angle from that of the house door, helps to keep out draughts. Draught proofing of all doors is essential and really good double glazing makes all the difference between a warm habitable house and an impossible one, and saves fuel by the ton. Double glazing also reduces noise by providing an insulating layer, but the panes need to be about 3 to 4in apart to achieve quietness. This could be important near the sea.

Few seaside houses or cottages (outside towns and big villages) have gas. Electric central heating by storage heaters is expensive and rather inflexible, not being capable of instant use. Oil-fired central heating relies upon fuel deliveries as does solid fuel heating. Scandinavian and other woodburning stoves, based on traditional and proven designs, are just about the most effective way to warm small houses provided you have a source of wood fuel. They burn almost any wood and are quite happy to consume large chunks of beach timber, salt and all, if it is available. They are fairly expensive to install but once in, need no maintenance beyond a weekly clean out and refuelling twice or three times a day. Free standing in the middle of the room if necessary with (expensive) chimney flues up through the rest of the house, exuding warmth, they shimmer with heat and can do a certain amount of simmering and cooking. Some styles can be opened up so that one has the cheerful benefit of seeing the flames.

Solar panels, properly installed on a roof, working in conjunction with an electric immersion heater provide cheap hot water. Over the course of a year, four solar heating panels should save about one third of the normal cost of providing domestic water, and in summertime, provided we get average amounts of sunshine, very little electricity indeed is needed to back up the solar heat. Even in our climate which does not provide perpetual sunshine the amount of heat to be gained from solar heating installations is considerably more than most people who have no experience of it, find it possible to believe. Those who have it seem to be very pleased with it. The cost of installation is not high, and the saving on fuel costs will certainly be more than the interest on the capital expenditure, so there must be a considerable net saving.

Existing patterns of solar panels are reasonably efficient heat collectors, but as development continues there will undoubtedly be technological advances and the panels will be made of materials with higher heat absorption properties than at present. When that day comes, solar heating for dwelling houses will change all present concepts of domestic water heating.

Houseboats

For many people there would seem to be no pleasanter way to live by tidal waters, than actually to live on them in a houseboat, and in fact about 15,000 people in Britain do, although most of them are moored on rivers and lakes and non-tidal waters. But wherever there are estuaries and big natural harbours, there are houseboats. Houseboats on tidal water go up and down with the tide, unless they are in such a bad state that their bottoms remain firmly on the mud and the water

221

A small modern houseboat – the marine equivalent of a caravan *(A. E. Coe)*

just rises and falls up and down their hulls. Their inhabitants love the continual change from water and its noise and movement to mudflat with its seabirds and waders.

LAW AND HOUSEBOATS

After the war the government actually encouraged people to buy up old Motor Torpedo boats and suchlike, and convert them into houseboats, and even issued helpful instructions. Many an old fishing boat or barge has been converted to a sound and roomy houseboat. However, when you really go deeply into the subject you discover some unpleasant facts. Firstly there is practically no law specifically relating to houseboats, so that even the definition of what is or is not a houseboat is questionable. A boat that cannot move under its own power is accepted to be a houseboat, or any boat that has not moved from its moorings for three years. Yet thousands of people live in houseboats which can uphook and chunter off to other locations or even go on cruises. Some live full time on what are fully operational and registered yachts, either sail or motor or both.

Owners of moored yachts are not expected to pay rates, neither are the boats expected to be lived in or remain semi-permanently at their moorings, so if you lay down permanent moorings, sink piles to keep your boat in position, add permanent walkways or gangways, the local authority may ask you to pay rates, even though you do not own the land alongside which you are moored. That they should then provide a water supply and refuse collection, if you pay rates, does not always suit them.

Most people own their boats, but must rent somewhere to moor. Lucky the person who actually owns the land against which he is moored, and has got the necessary planning permission to erect permanent walkways, etc. Caravan owners are in a similar position but while there are three Acts of Parliament covering mobile homes on land, there is none for mobile homes on water, and residential boats were specifically excluded from the Government's recent Mobile Homes Review.

So, if you fancy a houseboat, be very careful. First of all you must have a mooring, and security of tenure. Secondly, if you wish to buy a boat already on a mooring, you must be sure that it has a lease, and security of tenure. Check with the local authority and river or harbour board. Unfortunately you may meet with a lot of obstructive discouragement. There are some local authorities who encourage houseboats, and go to great lengths to provide mains services, sewage disposal, etc, but they are the exception rather than the rule, and in many areas definite efforts are being made to get rid of houseboats.

About the only concession that has been made to the houseboat owner is that if he is rendered homeless because he has been turfed off his mooring, then accommodation must be found for him under the Housing (Homeless Persons) Act 1977, but this does not mean that another mooring must be found, just that he must be offered a roof over his head.

There is no rent control mechanism so you can be charged what the owner of the land likes, and no rent or rates rebates or home improvement grants are available. There is no control over the terms of a mooring agreement so landlords can do what they like and craft can be evicted; and there is no appeal and no compensation.

As an example of the total lack of legal protection, one man who tried to get legal aid to fight a case to do with his houseboat, was refused, initially, on the grounds that as there was no houseboat

'J' class yacht, *Mariquita*, has been a houseboat for many years

Old barge converted into houseboat

legislation he could not win the case, so there was no point in giving him legal aid!

All this may sound archaic and astonishing in this day and age when those who rent homes on land are protected to the point of stupidity.

The Residential Boat Owners Association has tried and is trying very hard to get a Bill on to the Statute Book which would give houseboat owners 'Security of tenure in the same spirit as the Caravan Acts of 1960 and 1968 . . . and the Rent Act 1965'. Meanwhile the Association is extremely active, doing everything it can to help members in trouble and to lobby MPs and take up all the cases of injustice and hardship wherever they happen. Houseboaters come from all walks of life so there is plenty of ability and expertise to carry on the battle. Battle it is, because it is quite extraordinary how in some areas local councils and other residents resent the houseboats, claiming, usually, that they are a blot on the landscape, pollute their surroundings, and should be got rid of.

The continuing and increasing interest in and use of our inland waterways is sparking off a much closer look by the authorities. In the long run it will produce legislation. It is not likely that they can get rid of all the houseboats, or even of those which they believe constitute a nuisance or interference with their plans in some way. Quite apart from anything else, housing is in short supply and yet would have to be found for the displaced, and the revenue from houseboaters is not to be sneezed at. Many people are prepared to pay substantial rents in return for reasonable leases, security of tenure, good facilities and surroundings, and tidy neighbours, and where houseboats are encouraged, local councillors are well aware of this. Nevertheless it is an undoubted fact that all too many houseboats not in marinas are in a shocking state and are nothing but slums. They spoil it for the rest of course; but where local branches of the RBOA exist great efforts are made to tidy things up so that this charge of slumminess cannot be raised.

TYPES OF BOAT

Yachts can be bought on mortgage being subject to registration, but houseboats are not regarded by the law as homes but as chattels so do not rate for mortgage. Nevertheless one can buy magnificent custom-built houseboats which are really flats or large caravans on a substantial raft, and some companies are prepared to give mortgages on these if they are fully convinced that the mortgagee has plenty of security.

There are many types of houseboat and adverts can be found in boating magazines and in, for instance, *Exchange and Mart* for all sorts of houseboats. Many are conversions, some small and ancient and tatty, some large and palatial, some large and dilapidated, some tiny, tight and delightful, and some custom built on their own rafts.

CHECKING A BOAT

Never buy a houseboat without having it thoroughly surveyed by a competent marine surveyor. Water moves, tidal or not, and anything on it, however solid, must also move. It is this movement which causes trouble. Examine the boat at high tide when it should be floating and make sure that no water is getting into the bilges anywhere. Examine it at low tide to make sure that no water is coming out of it where it should not. Continual leakage in or out leaves marks and traces. Boats in fresh water rot more quickly than boats in salt water, but marine organisms can colonise the bottom of a boat and eventually cause damage. Decks work as the boat moves, so see the boat in pouring rain in case the deck leaks. Houseboat owners fight a constant battle against deck leakage because new leaks appear all the

Houseboats can travel *(A. E. Coe)*

time. Glass fibre and other fillers developed in recent years have made a big difference to the possibilities of repair. But whatever the condition of the boat, maintenance costs will be high, and you must be prepared to work constantly to keep the boat in good repair.

Check electrical wiring if any. Where wires pass through bilges or anywhere where water may get at them, they are vulnerable for even the best insulation gives out eventually. Boats, although surrounded by water, are extremely inflammable, so check anything that might be a fire risk.

Any kind of heating as used on shore may be used in a houseboat, provided it is properly installed, but gas or solid fuel stoves which give off fumes must have proper ventilation because, especially in winter and bad weather, the boat may be tightly shut to keep out weather and conserve heat. Double glazing wherever possible is a necessity, not only to keep in heat but to cut down condensation which is always a source of trouble in boats. Look for damage caused by condensation especially in galleys, and bathrooms and toilets. The hull is in contact outside with cold water, so is cool on its inside, and therefore any steam, from bath or breath or tea-kettle, causes condensation. There are special anti-condensation paints, but double skinning is the best answer: double glazed windows and an interior skin with a cavity between it and the hull. Polystyrene foam is an excellent insulating and condensation-preventing material, but it is also extremely inflammable and gives off choking and dangerous black smoke when set on fire, so beware of it.

FIRE PRECAUTIONS

A houseboat should have firefighting appliances. A bucket on a rope can be kept on deck where it can conveniently be dropped over the side to get water to fight a fire. Powder extinguishers are excellent, and foam extinguishers the best of all, even though they do make a mess. Better a boat saved in a mess than a boat burned. Keep a bucket of sand in the galley, or a fire-blanket sold specifically for the purpose; which is excellent for putting out a chip-pan fire or a small petrol or spirit fire. Prevention is best, so inspect a boat carefully to see that the siting of stoves, heaters, flues, fuel tanks, gas bottles, in fact anything which could cause fires, is sensible and in perfect order. The water authorities regulations governing boats state that fuel tanks and fuel gas pipes must be made of materials that are not likely to melt if a fire starts. For instance, if the engine backfires through an unguarded carburettor and it catches fire, a plastic fuel line melts very quickly and fuel runs into the fire; copper does not melt immediately and the fire burns itself out before it gets hot enough to melt the copper. Soldered joints melt, but compression joints do not. Pipes should be properly curved and bent rather than cut and jointed, wherever possible, Leaking gas, being heavier than air, runs down into the bilges and builds up until one day it ignites. Petrol is so inflammable that if the vapour is blowing in a breeze from an uncapped tank, it can ignite from a cigarette being smoked 60 yards away.

A CO_2 extinguisher puts out electrical fires and fires in enclosed spaces by displacing all the air, and thus starving the fire of oxygen. If you set one off, batten down the hatches and stay on the outside.

In any case of fire, send for the Fire Brigade, for even if the fire appears to be out it is best to have the boat checked by expert firefighters in case there is a chance of the thing re-igniting later on.

MOORINGS

Houseboats are usually moored in groups, rarely on their own, and nowhere except in a caravan park can you find yourself more cheek by jowl with the neighbours. So it is important when deciding on a mooring, or buying a boat already on mooring, to consider the neighbours. If you are not going to get on with them, or intend to be a solitary, or at least not become part of the community, then problems loom. You will be sharing sewage- and waste-disposal points, be on the same little branch of mains supplies, and inevitably overlook one another. In organised houseboat marinas, the boats should be moored

Houseboat moorings attached to convenient tree

so that no one has to cross anyone else's deck, garden or gangplank to reach their own boat; an echelon formation is the best way to moor the greatest number of boats in a given space. This formation requires a bank or a hard, and one pile or dolphin per boat to hold the other end. This system may not be effective where there is much fall of tide as the boats will end up on a sloping bottom at low water unless they have legs or special pilings to prevent this. The best system is that of floating trots. Piles are driven into the river or sea bed and floating pontoons, which move up and down them, provide walkways and mooring platforms to which each boat can be moored fore and aft. Linking spine walkways give access to the bank, and metered electricity and water supplies can be taken easily to each boat.

Beware of boats moored alongside a bank with outer boats moored to them. The outside residents must cross the inner boats to reach the bank, especially in tidal waters or where levels may produce problems of access. It is not easy to carry mains services to the outer boats.

FURTHER READING   Powell, Audrey. *Your Holiday Home* (David & Charles); McKnight, Hugh. *The Shell Book of Inland Waterways* (David & Charles); Hadfield, Charles. *Introducing Inland Waterways* (David & Charles); Marriott, Hugh. *Owning A Boat* (Nautical Pub).

HOUSEBOAT BUILDERS   *Windboats Marine Ltd,* Wroxham, Norwich, Norfolk NR12 8RX; *S. Theunissen,* Willowwren Wharf, Southall, Middx.

USEFUL ADDRESSES   *Inland Waterways Asscn,* 114 Regents Park Road, London NW1; *The Residential Boat Owners Asscn* Hon Sec Mrs B. Stainer, N/B Eridanus, Benbow Way Moorings, Cowley, Middx.

15

Plants

Gardening in Coastal Areas

Wind, salt and sand are the enemies of the seaside gardener. However, close to the coast, frosts are not usually so severe as they are inland, and in high rainfall areas the coast has several inches a year less rain than its hinterland. Your winter weather very much depends on where you live. All down the north and east coasts, the vicious winds off the sea coming down unchecked from the Arctic Circle, play havoc with plants and shrubs, and the cold and salt deposited on their leaves kills and scorches all but the hardiest. Right on until May the winds are biting and dry. Low-level gardens anywhere right down by the shore also suffer badly from the blasting of wind-blown sand. The light along the south coast is good, and the winds are nothing like so cold or severe, nor so dry, and south-facing gardens benefit from some sunshine all the year round. In the South West and along the west coast the air is balmy and humid even in summer, and in winter it is extremely wet, but there is nothing like so much frost or severe cold. Instead the severe Atlantic gales can physically uproot anything in their path. Look at the flattened and eastward-leaning scrub oak trees in the hedgerows of North Cornwall and the shapes of entire hedges, where they exist at all, on our really exposed western coasts and you will see what I mean.

On the south and west coasts, partly because of the warmth and moisture brought by the Gulf Stream, there is no reason why in gardens either naturally or artificially sheltered from the wind, you should not be able to grow an enormous range of plants, provided they like your soil. All along the south coast, and out to the Scilly Isles (swept by westerly gales) palms and other subtropical plants thrive.

A seaside garden must have shelterbelts, either some that grow quickly or that are easy to put up. It has been proved that solid walls

230

and fences are not ideal shelters because the wind curls over on the leeward side causing much turbulence, whereas permeable screening allows the wind to pass through without excess turbulence, but reduces its force enormously. The most recent development is made of hanging strips of plastic, now being widely used in Holland to protect crops from the wind. This is put up right round the plot and creates a cage of undisturbed air. The principle could be applied to decorative gardens but would rather spoil their looks. For vegetable gardens it could be an ideal solution.

Lath fences erected on solid posts and cross members break the wind for a distance up to twenty times the height of the screen, but are only fully effective for about a third of that distance. Thus a 4ft fence shelters about 30ft of ground behind it. The laths are fixed about 1in apart.

Fences and walls round seaside gardens are a problem. Impermeable wooden fencing, either weather-board on rails or the cheaper types made of interwoven thin slats, presents too solid a surface to the wind and there is no type of post that will hold it for long in really exposed places. Wooden posts in holes in the ground loosen with continual wind movement, and if set in concrete will eventually rot and snap off. Even concrete posts crack under the terrific pressure of the wind. Solid walls stay put, but as described above, cause turbulence. My grand-mother's seaside garden on the north Norfolk coast had a flint wall about 3ft high on top of which was another 3ft of wattle fencing. It was a magnificent garden, so presumably the openwork wattle provided a good windbreak above the wall and thus reduced the turbulence at its base, in its lee.

Lath screens will not last for ever, so it is good sense to plant shrubs behind to form a permanent shelterbelt. There are many suitable shrubs, but it does depend on how near sea level the garden is. Tamarisk and sea buckthorn grow in almost pure sand and resist all wind-blown salt water. Take advice from your local nurseryman on suitability. On colder coasts plants must also be able to stand up to biting winds. Gorse grows on cliffs almost anywhere, self seeds (which can be a nuisance) and forms bright and solid hedges which small birds love for shelter. Bush lupins grow fast and well and produce masses of lemon-yellow flowers. They self seed prolifically. I have seen these lupins apparently completely killed by salt-water flooding grow again from their roots during the following summer. The original bushes always die off after a few years but should have replaced themselves with self-sown bushes. They are best planted where they have room to do this, and not in neat regimented hedgerows.

If higher shelter is needed, plant trees as soon as the bushes are established, quick or slow growing as you choose. *Cupresso cyparis leylandii* is the most popular quick-growing hedge tree, and has been developed for that purpose. Four feet a year is as good as one can get, and if pruned it makes good thick hedges, or can be allowed to grow up into tall trees. Salt-laden wind scorches it, so it cannot be used on a totally exposed site without itself having some shelter. Use small plants, not big ones, both of trees and shrubs; shelter them and they will grow very fast, as they are less liable to wind damage than big plants.

Vegetables by the Sea

Just as much if not more of a problem than growing flowers, seaside vegetable gardening can be heartbreaking. Shelter is essential. Vegetables need a lot of water, and it must be available. The sandier or lighter the soil the less moisture it retains; remember how beach sand dries out where the sea does not reach it. Have some type of mains-connected sprinkler if possible. To retain moisture the soil must contain humus. The problem of humus in seaside soils, not only sand, but in light thin soils over wind-scoured rock, has always beset those trying to crop them. Traditionally tons and tons of seaweed were harvested to improve soil character and fertilise it. Nowadays artificials provide the nutrients, but the soil character may still be wrong. If seaweed is available then collect it, hose it down thoroughly with fresh water to get rid of most of the salt, then dig it into the ground or use it in layers in a compost heap. As it takes some time to rot down, seaweed should be dug in after clearing the ground in the autumn, and as long as possible before the ground is to be reused. Of course use as much compost and mulch as possible. Mulching with peat holds surface moisture, and it eventually goes into the soil providing humus.

Do not grow tall vegetables in windy gardens. There are plenty of excellent dwarf varieties available of almost everything, and ground-hugging plants such as marrows or courgettes do well on good soil. Plant your seeds and seedlings as close together as possible to squeeze out the wind, and use cloches to provide shelter.

Rows of bean poles provide a nice target for the wind, but a screen of solid plastic mesh tacked on to end posts well dug into the ground and tamped in with stones, or driven in, provides a less easily uprooted

Edible seakale *(Crambe maritima)*

Edible cliff cabbage *(Brassica cleracea)*

base, although the dwarf varieties are safer. Such hardy vegetables as Jerusalem artichokes can be grown as a shelter hedge, but they do tend to take over unless firmly dug back each year. They produce an enormous crop which you could sell if you hate the things as much as I do.

ASPARAGUS

Asparagus thrives by the sea because it likes well-drained sandy soil and tolerates a certain amount of salt. To make an asparagus bed, dig a 3ft trench and bury plenty of compost or farmyard manure 2ft down. Add a layer of rotted seaweed and replace the soil. Add a generous amount of general fertiliser to the topsoil, about 4oz per sq yd. In late March or early April plant 1- or 2-year-old asparagus crowns, 1½ft apart in 2 rows 4ft apart. Make holes 6 to 8in deep and place the plants in with the roots fanned out, about 4in below the surface. Do not crop at all in the first year but in the autumn, when the ferns begin to turn colour, cut them off to within an inch of the ground, mulch well and leave till the spring. Then in March apply another top dressing of general fertiliser, and if you wish the asparagus to be blanched, add about 3in of topsoil in a ridge over the plants. Crop lightly the second year. After the end of June leave the plants to develop into fern. Too heavy cropping will reduce the size of next year's crop.

HERBS

Most herbs like semi-sheltered places, not too sunny, not too shady, not too dry and not too wet, and prefer to be left to grow naturally, more or less unchecked. Thyme which grows wild on chalk downs, takes to chalky, gravelly, light soil. So do marjoram, juniper, hyssop, tarragon, chervil, and rosemary. Most other herbs prefer richer soil, well drained but moist. It may be best to grow your herbs first in pots, planting them out with the soil still round the roots, and adding spadesful of light loamy soil to make a little bed for each plant. Once established most herbs will grow well if kept lightly watered and sheltered from cold winds and blazing sunshine.

Greenhouses

Put your greenhouse in a sheltered place or fierce winds will not only force draughts into it and fling shingle to break the glass, but the chill factor of the wind will render it almost useless in winter if unheated, and is bound to put up heating costs. Make sure the greenhouse is

Sea holly *(Erynqium maritimum)* has beautiful pale green and blue leaves with blue flowers

really well anchored, and set up with the door facing away from the prevailing wind.

Flowers

Given enough shelter, almost anything can be grown, but tall plants are very vulnerable to the wind; lupins, delphiniums, etc, must be well staked if they are to stand up. Plants which naturally grow by the sea, pinks, carnations, mesembryanthemums, and many others, can be most successful.

Wild Flowers and Plants

I possess an old book *Flowers and Ferns of Cromer and its Neighbourhood*. It describes a series of walks, really. The writer obviously spent years in the district, walking its fields, woods, heaths, cliffs, beaches and saltmarshes, listing the plants that grew there. This is my home, and I too used to find some of the same plants in those same habitats. Yet now where once the cornfields were full of scarlet poppies, and the hedges yellow with primroses, only a neat green chemically controlled countryside remains. The woodland primroses have been over-picked and destroyed, and for the same two reasons, chemicals and collectors, the orchids have gone from the meadows.

Fortunately, here as elsewhere round our coasts, the plants of cliff, shingle bank and saltmarsh have survived because these habitats remain almost untouched by the chemical sprays and because many of these areas are protected and watched over by conservationists. The rare plants survive and the common ones spread. So for the botanist and flower lover these places are marvellously productive.

The edible plants do grow in profusion so there is no harm in picking and eating them. Nevertheless never pick them where there are only a few plants.

The flowers and grasses which grow in sand dunes should be left undisturbed for they are performing the vital functions of binding the sand, and making humus to increase its fertility and moisture-holding properties. This encourages further growth and eventually allows the establishment of bigger plants, bushes and grasses to provide habitats for birds and small mammals.

Of course beaches which are continuously washed by the sea do not grow plants, and the high spring tide mark is clearly enough the point where the land plants cease. Yet where only occasional floods or surges submerge them, it is surprising how those plants with their roots in sand or shingle do survive to grow again, and how their seeds germinate and flourish although one would have thought them to have been completely washed away or ruined.

Study the plants which grow in a particular habitat with a notebook and camera, or study the effects of high tides and other unusual things upon the flora of an area. Where an area of grass among sand dunes has been accidentally burnt, the plants that regrow immediately and the seeds that germinate in due course can provide quite a surprise. I know one area where asparagus grows wild, in scattered clumps among thickly matted grass, behind low sand dunes. An acre or so of this grass was burned during the growing season; that night it rained, and two days later there was such a crop of perfect asparagus over the whole area that we could pick pounds and pounds of it, where before that there had only been a few crowns. Obviously the long-established crowns had many runners underground which were not capable of pushing shoots up through the thick grass and its roots. When the cover was burned away along with the top layer of roots, the rain in the fire-warmed earth stimulated this asparagus to rapid growth. Over the same area, in the following year, yellow and white melilot germinated and grew in a 3ft-high forest, the seed thriving where the competition from the grass was eliminated. This same sweet-smelling melilot also grows and thrives in the dunes swept during the previous winter by at least one flood tide.

Early this year a North Sea surge completely flattened a mile or so of shingle bank and spread it over the first 70 or 80 yards of a golf course behind. This shingle, which had never grown much more than a rough crop of ragwort, thistles and grass, was bulldozed back into place as a bare level bank. Within a few weeks plants began to germinate and in the spring it was a green carpet. The inevitable willow herb which always appears where ground has been burned or laid waste, grew, and so did every other plant which had ever been there. Presumably there were thousands of dormant seeds which enjoyed being bulldozed up to the surface of freshly disturbed shingle.

Further back there were many thriving bush lupins, which had been deliberately planted a few years before to brighten the place up. The flood of sea water shrivelled them all, and in the spring it looked as if they had completely 'had it'. But during the summer, from deep down in the bottoms of the woody stems, new shoots began to appear, and by next year it looks as if there will again be lush lupins in flower.

Saltmarshes carry tremendous amounts of vegetation which enjoy the silt of their estuaries, and many of the plants, such as samphire, suffer partial immersion at every spring tide, and thrive on it.

Edible Plants

SAMPHIRE

True samphire, *crithmum maritimum,* grows on sea cliffs and dry saltmarshes, and is only common locally. It grows to about 1ft high and is rather grey looking (so many plants which survive well in salt air are greyish in colour), but has yellow daisy-like flowers. It has thick fleshy leaves and solid stems which can be eaten, and smells not unlike salty, oily celery. Samphire is usually eaten fresh in a salad or pickled in vinegar.

Pickled Samphire

samphire	chillies
vinegar	sprig of thyme
small white onions, peeled	cloves
salt	

Clean and trim the samphire and soak it in water for 24 hours. Drain and wipe it well with a cloth. Put the samphire in a large bowl, covered with vinegar which has been boiled. Leave it to steep for 10 hours. Drain off the vinegar, reboil it with more fresh vinegar, allowing $\frac{1}{2}$ pint fresh to every 3 pints of boiled vinegar. Pour all this boiling vinegar over the samphire. Drain the samphire after a few minutes, put in jars with small white onions, a few chillies, a sprig of thyme, some cloves and a pinch of salt, and cover these all with the vinegar. Seal the jars carefully.

MARSH SAMPHIRE OR GLASSWORT
This is *salicornia stricta* and grows in great meadows on firm mud, usually in saltmarshes, and is under water at high tide. In July when it is at its best it is vivid green, growing darker and redder in August/September. It looks like little cacti with lobed branches. Pick the samphire from areas where the tide has washed the plants well. Wash it in fresh water and pick out any weeds and roots.

Pickled Samphire
Cut off the roots and wash the samphire. Cook it in water with about 2 tablespoons of vinegar, bringing it slowly to the boil. Take the samphire off the stove while it is still green and crisp. Put it into Kilner jars, pour on the vinegar and seal the jars tightly. It can be eaten straightaway or kept for a few months.

Buttered Samphire

marsh samphire	salt and pepper
water	butter

Wash the plants thoroughly in several rinses of cold water. Put them in a saucepan and cover with water. Boil them for 20 minutes until the fleshy parts slip easily off the stalks. Drain them, season with salt and pepper and serve piping hot with melted butter.

Eat the samphire by picking up each piece and sucking it. A hot plate is useful when serving it, because samphire takes time to eat and gets cold rather quickly.

It is equally tasty eaten cold dipped in home-made mayonnaise or sprinkled with a little lemon juice, oil and vinegar.

Samphire in Cream
Cook as in Buttered Samphire, then drain the water off and dry the

238

samphire in a cloth. Heat a little butter in a pan and toss the samphire in this for a few minutes, then add double cream and simmer for a couple more minutes. Season and serve very hot.

SEAKALE

Crambe maritima is very common indeed in some places, on shingle by the sea. All round the great shingle point of Dungeness, seakale pushes up through the shingle in dark purplish red sprouts in spring, and grows into big tussocky green bushes as the summer comes, to disappear eventually in winter. At all times the vegetable makes good eating. In spring the little tender sprouts cooked for 10 minutes in salted water and served with plenty of melted butter make a wonderful vegetable with roast meat, or even a dish by themselves, like asparagus. Later the newest green shoots from the centres of the plants are equally good as a vegetable. The taste and crisp texture of seakale make it an unusual delicacy.

CLIFF CABBAGE

Around the south-eastern corner of England, on the white cliffs of Dover, grows wild *brassica oleracea,* another rather salty delicacy, especially when the purplish green sprouts are picked fresh in the spring. This plant is reputed to be an escapee from Roman kitchen gardens, and the ancestor of our domestic cabbage, originating therefore in the Mediterranean. Whatever the truth of this story, cliff cabbage is well worth eating and perhaps deep-freezing for winter use.

SEA BEET

'Beta' vulgaris grows just above the high tide line on shingle, or just above the spray line on cliffs. It rather likes rough disturbed ground and can be found almost anywhere near the sea, perhaps at the edges of car parks and caravan sites. It is an ugly sprawling plant with dark green, hairless, shiny, leathery leaves, which nevertheless can be washed, cooked and eaten like spinach.

Edible seaweeds

Seaweeds are a health-giving source of natural iodine, but are a rather acquired taste.

LAVER AND SEA LETTUCE

In Scotland laver is known as sloke. There are two types of laver.

Green laver, *ulva lactua,* is a bright green, thin, but wide leaf, growing in rock pools left by the low tide; it can be gathered and eaten at all times of the year. Pick off the dark stem pieces, wash thoroughly and boil for 20 minutes, serve with salt, lemon or vinegar. It tastes a little like delicate cabbage.

The purple laver which is gathered to make laverbread, is a far tastier plant. *Porphyria umbilicalis* grows abundantly on rocky shores. It is a rich purple colour and grows in rock pools. It is best picked in early spring, and should be laid out to dry on a sandy floor under cover, but where the air can flow over it. Turn it daily. If you do not wish to dry the laver, just soak it thoroughly for a few hours in cold water with a little bicarbonate of soda, drain and cook immediately. The best laverbread is made from dried laver, and it is said that it takes seven years for the drying floor to develop the proper bacteria to give the seaweed its full flavour.

Wash the dried seaweed carefully to get rid of sand, then steep it in cold fresh water with a little bicarbonate of soda added. This gets rid of a certain bitterness. Strain, and cover with fresh water in a heavy pan; simmer it till it becomes almost a jelly, very dark greenish black in colour. Put it in an earthenware jar, where it will keep for two or three weeks. It can be eaten spread on bread or oatcakes, or mixed with oatmeal to make little flat cakes which are fried with bacon and eggs. Mixed with pepper and lemon juice or orange juice, it makes an excellent sauce for roast mutton.

Another way to make laver sauce for roast lamb or venison is to boil together the juice of 2 lemons, 1 tablespoon of redcurrant jelly, 4 tablespoons of beef stock or gravy, and a pinch of caster sugar, for 10 minutes. Skim, add ½ pint of cooked laverbread and boil all together again. Put through a blender and serve hot.

CARRAGHEEN OR SEA MOSS

In Ireland and the Hebrides *chondrus crispus* grows abundantly on rocky shores. Gather, clip off the roots and dark stems, and spread it out in showery weather. It changes colour to creamy white and can then be brought indoors to dry out quickly on a sunny windowsill. When it is dry it can be stored. To use carragheen, wash half an ounce of the dried seaweed, and steep it in fresh water for 30 minutes. Then boil it in a saucepan for 20 minutes with 1½ pints of milk and some pieces of lemon rind. It will go thick and custardy and you should then add sugar to taste, and stir in a well-beaten egg, but do not reboil. The mixture can then be strained into a mould and left in the refrigerator to set. Serve with slightly sour cream or natural yoghurt. This makes a most unusual dessert.

FURTHER READING   Martin, Keble. *The Concise British Flora* (Michael Joseph); Kelway, C. *Seaside Gardening; Gardening on the Coast* and *Gardening on Sand* (David & Charles); McClintock, and Fitter, *Collins Pocket Guide to Wild Flowers* (Collins); Fitter, R. S. R. *Finding Wild Flowers* (Collins).

16

Round the Coast

To give any real idea of what any part of our varied coastline is like, for those who do not know it, takes thousands of words and hundreds of pictures. Television has made a lot of it, if not familiar, at least not totally strange.

The coastline of Great Britain is 6,000 miles long. That is a startling statistic, and is I suppose how far you would walk if you started at A and went along every inch of beach and cliff, up one side of each estuary and down the other, and so on back to A. Even if you cut the corners and ferried across the estuaries, it would still work out at 4 or 5 thousand miles. We have a population of 60 million, give or take a few, to go with that 6,000 miles, so that every member of the population could stand side by side and line the island like sailors dressing ship, if they wanted to. Luckily, because not everyone goes to the coast at the same time, and because by far the majority of those who do, congregate in large or small clusters, and only do that in the summer, there are hundreds of miles of empty coastline. Some of it is inaccessible except on foot, some of it is used by the Services as firing and bombing ranges. The regulations vary for these areas, and some are completely closed, others open at specified times. Whatever the rules, obey them and do not stray on land or on water, into possible danger. Large areas of the south-west coast, and of the Welsh coast are restricted in this way.

Great stretches of our coastline remain empty because over the centuries population and development centred round the navigable estuaries, and cities, such as London, Southampton and Portsmouth, Plymouth, Bristol, Liverpool, Glasgow, Newcastle and Hull, formed the main coastal centres of population. Other fishing ports big and small made up the rest of the towns, and until this century there was not much else on the coast. Now we have the resorts which built up

The varied coast of Britain: the Sound of Sleat between Glenelg and Skye (inhabited by thousands of cormorants and eider duck) contrasts strongly with – Sandwich Bay, lovely in its utterly different way

usually round small fishing villages, some fading or at least remaining static as more and more people go abroad for holidays, others such as the enormous development of Brighton and its neighbouring towns stretching without a break from Peacehaven to Littlehampton. This is one of the favourite retirement areas, and Brighton as its centre has developed into a kind of London by the sea, with marvellous shops, a University, and full entertainment facilities.

For holidays, sand dunes are not popular if they are of any size because it is hard to struggle on foot through soft sand carrying beach gear. Shingle banks attract fishermen, but, unless there is sand at low water, repel families because children hate them, being hard on bare feet and not much use for bucket and spade. Cliffs, whether chalky or sandy or rocky, have to be negotiated, and in hot weather that can be a bind. Most people arrive by car or coach, so car parks have become part of the beach scene. Caravan parks are necessary for the itinerant and the temporary seaside resident. Seaside estates suit those who prefer reasonable shopping and other facilities. Established ports and resorts of all sizes suit those who like town life by the sea. There are very few seaside villages left which, especially in the South, South West and West, do not have their proportion of incomers, either full-time or weekend and holiday residents. Only in the most inaccessible areas are there many old cottages left for restoration and conversion. Prices are high in direct ratio to the proximity of cities (for which neighbouring coastal towns and villages are dormitories) and yachting harbours. A main line railway to the nearest big city or to London puts up property prices. In some areas such as north Norfolk, the very fact that the railway line has been closed actually put up prices because it remains without major roads and is unspoiled.

Most of the estuaries where there are small ports and villages, in other words where access from the sea is not too difficult for cruising boats, and where there is sailing water at high tide, are expanding rapidly in terms of sailing population. Most estuaries have areas favoured by seabirds and waders and migrants, especially in winter. The National Trust and other conservationist societies control and protect a lot of them, but more protection is needed. It is true to say that every estuary of natural beauty is already colonised by humans, and cottages are not easy to come by. Only the wildest, bleakest and most inaccessible are comparatively empty.

(*Opposite*)
Sunlight on the sand at low tide. It could be on the coast or in an estuary

The south coast from Chichester to Poole and the Isle of Wight, include our most popular (and expensive) sailing harbours and waters, but regionally many others are important. The Essex estuaries, the Menai Straits and the mouth of the Clyde have always been popular, but everywhere a boat can float, or find safe moorings, sailing thrives, and nowhere on the coast is one very far from sailing water. Round the rugged westerly and along the lonely north-east coasts, small boats are limited to staying inside the bays, estuaries and harbours.

There are designated cliff walks round the south-western peninsula of Devon and Cornwall, and Wales, and others are planned. For those who love walking and magnificent sea and cliff scenery, then there are hundreds of miles of western coastline to explore.

For bird watchers and botanists there are the sand flats and salt-marshes not only of north Norfolk and south-east Essex, but in almost every estuary large or small, there are bird sanctuaries and preservation areas.

The cold north and east coasts have their holiday resorts but they also have miles of cliffs, not quite so beautiful as the west coast, but often wilder and more remote. There are also hundreds of miles of sand and sand dunes, long open beaches, bleak in winter but beautiful in summer. There are some industrial towns along the north coast and some fishing ports.

Yet the only way to find out about these places is to go and look for yourself; so take all these factors into account, study maps and guide books, and go and explore the areas that appeal to you. Then for the really determined it is always possible to find somewhere to live.

Consider the coastline climatically, generally speaking. The whole of the north and east coast is bitterly cold in winter, because the north-easterly wind comes straight down from the Arctic Circle without interruption. Spring comes late and summers are short. But rainfall is slight, nowhere more than 30in per annum, often less then 25in. That includes snowfall, not usually so heavy down the east coast. The west coast is wet and windy in winter, swept bare by the prevailing westerlies coming ahead of Atlantic depressions. Full of rain, picked up from the sea, but much warmer than the east coast because of the warm Gulf Stream which swirls across the Atlantic and wraps the whole of Britain's west coast like a soggy blanket. Except in a few spots, the west-coast rainfall averages between 40 and 60in, only going higher where the high hills come near the sea. The big exception is the coastline between Llandudno on the North Wales coast and the top end of Morecambe Bay where it averages only 30 to 40in. Except

246

for the Cornish peninsula the south-coast rainfall is between 30 and 40in, with slightly less in the South East.

There are more thunderstorms in the eastern half of England. Thunderstorms drop a lot of rain at one time, so it follows that in addition to average rainfall being lower, a higher proportion of that comes in heavy thunder-showers rather than in steady drizzle. It takes a lot of West Country drizzle to make up for a few East Anglian tempests, and drizzle takes much longer to fall.

The basically triangular shape of our island does mean that the south coast gets the most sunshine. In terms of recorded hours it does, although the far north in summer has fantastically long days and light nights. Looking out across the North Sea the sun is somewhere over your right shoulder, and the sea looks quite unlike the English Channel or the Atlantic with the southerly or south-westerly sun behind it, back lighting the waves and ripples and reflecting straight into your eyes. I believe this is why the North Sea always looks so grey, except on calm days of high summer, and why the south and west coasts are so popular.

My daughter, home from New Zealand, said, 'The wonderful thing about Britain is its variety. In everything, people, places, architecture, countryside, coastline, climate, political parties, food, cities, clothes and culture. There is nowhere in the world like it.'

With 6,000 miles of coastline to choose from, who would want to live anywhere else?

FURTHER READING Seymour, John. 'Companion Guide' Series (Collins); Smith, Anthony and Southam, Jill. *Good Beach Guide* (Penguin).

Appendix

Coastal Archaeology

Though not strictly within the scope of a book about living by tidal waters, I cannot just ignore the dozens of castles and hundreds of other archaeological traces of our history which stud the coastline. Obviously, being an island opposite a continent, we were always subject to invasion from there and a great many castles were built to repel such invasion – not on a massive scale, but just as individual shelters for families, tribes or clans into which they could retreat and defend themselves. The Roman castles of the Saxon shore, such as Richborough, were built to provide protective forts for the invading troops, and others such as Henry II's Dover and Edward I's Welsh castles, to house a garrison which sallied forth to cope with either recalcitrant tribesmen or invading armies as the case might have been.

These islands were peopled by tribes or small nations who constantly attacked each other, especially after the Romans, who maintained some kind of unified control up to the Scottish border for 200 years, left for home. Most of the castles which remain were built after the Norman Conquest, and some such as Dover are in remarkable repair. All our history is in those castles and if you live near one it is impossible to ignore it and its historical implications.

I think the most important difference between, for instance, New Zealand and this country is that the former has no old buildings, no brick and stone history, and therefore no sense of permanence or continuity, so there is nothing to hold the eye and intellect except the physical look of the countryside and coastline. Only a forward-looking materialism concerns people, and there are no lessons to be learned from the future, and nothing remaining from past lessons to stimulate the mind or to guide it.

Plenty of fortifications and works designed to repel Napoleon,

Dover Castle

remain in the South East, notably the long line of martello towers.
Some of the pillboxes and gun emplacements remain from the two
great wars of our times, but none of them hold much history, and
those who remember the miles and miles of concrete and scaffolding
fences on all our vulnerable beaches and the minefields sown among
them, can only think of how comprehensively and quickly they were
removed.

The ancient ports and villages themselves continue a history which
was founded when men first began to settle in sheltered places by the
sea. The decline of many and the enormous expansion of a few,
because of changing coastlines or changing trades and changing means
of transport, is a fascinating study in itself and enough to keep one
going for years.

Nowhere else in the world is history still with us as it is in these
islands. Our very insularity preserved much of it from destruction by
invading armies. Most of our archives remain comparatively intact. It
is easy to take it for granted. Landing at Dover at night, the castle
stands floodlit on the cliff above the town, intact and looking as if it
was built yesterday, and few who glance at it do more than just that.
Not one in a million wonders what the ghost of that great king Henry
II thinks of 'Son et Lumiere'.

Index

252